Everything You Wanted to Know About **Phobias** But Were Afraid To Ask

Dr. Neal Olshan and Julie Wang

BEAUFORT BOOKS, INC.

New York / Toronto

Library of Congress Cataloging in Publication Data

Olshan, Neal.
  Everything you wanted to know about phobias but were afraid to ask.
  1. Phobias.   2. Desensitization [Psychotherapy]
I. Wang, Julie Dreyer. II. Title.
RC535.045   616.85'225   81-3843
                       AACR2
ISBN 0-8253-0073-8 [pbk.]

Published in the United States by Beaufort Books, Inc., New York.
Published simultaneously in Canada by Nelson, Foster and Scott Ltd.
Printed in the U.S.A.   First Beaufort Edition
10 9 8 7 6 5 4 3 2

Contents

Foreword

All of us, at one time or another, can benefit from a method to reduce fear, anxiety, and phobias. Whether the phobia has been present for ten years or two months makes little difference when the fear of an animal, airplane or making a speech causes you to suffer symptoms which can range from shaking to ulcers.

All the step-by-step procedures needed to rid yourself of crippling phobias are presented in a highly readable combination of self-help manual and exposition of phobias. First your phobias are identified and defined; then, by combining specific body control techniques with methods of visualizing the fearful situation, you will be able to break free from your phobias.

This is the first complete book to tell you how to end phobias and keep them from bothering you in the future.

PREFACE:
Assumptions of the Book

The case studies you will find in this book represent only a small number of the patients I have treated for phobias, but they constitute a cross-section of the wide variety of phobic reactions treated by my colleagues and myself. Over the past few decades behavioral scientists have developed treatment methods for helping people overcome their fears and phobias. These behavioral techniques are known by different names: behavior therapy, systematic desensitization, reciprocal inhibition, thought-stopping, role-playing and the program used in this book — fear reduction.

The fear reduction program is based on the idea that you can be trained through a re-learning process to overcome your phobic reactions. Since fear is a learned experience, it can also be unlearned, through the methods presented in this book. A major goal of this book is to help you define the fear reactions which can lead to phobic behavior. As you read through the information and begin the exercises you may notice your behavior gradually beginning to change.

The method of reducing your phobias is based on three assumptions, each of which is supported by many years of research and development by outstanding behavioral scientists throughout the world.

The first basic assumption is that:

YOU CAN CHANGE

All too often people fail to accept the responsibility for change within their own lives. They truly believe that there is no chance for significant change, and thereby sentence themselves to a life of unsatisfying feelings and emotions. Unfortunately, people tend to explain away their phobias by saying, "I've always been scared of such and such and I guess I always will be." This is very common, but you should take heart from hundreds of patients who have used the fear reduction program to overcome their phobias.

Change is possible if you actively seek it. If you truly believe that your situation can be changed, then the chances are very good that you will be able to modify the behavior that is bothering you.

The second assumption is:

MANY CHANGES CAN BE QUICK AND PERMANENT

It is not necessary to devote half your life to producing a change in behavior. Many of the changes brought about by the fear reduction program can be accomplished in a relatively short period of time. If you continue to practice the principles of the program the change can be permanent. You will be interested to learn that these principles are fairly simple, and putting them into practice can be fun.

I have said that change can be quick and permanent, but don't be deceived into thinking that you can change overnight. Changing your behaviors has to be a steady and planned process. Ending fears and phobias which have plagued you for years can't be accomplished in an hour or two. You may have taken years to develop a non-productive pattern of behavior and it will take time to reverse.

The time needed to change your behavior will be, in part, up to you. Some people are able to accomplish the reversal within a matter of a week to a week and a half. Others may take as long as four to six weeks. The length of time you take to change is no reflection of your intellectual abilities or the type of person you are. It simply means that some people have more time to practice and are more responsive to the techniques. The book outlines a gradual, yet steady reversal process. "Quickie" therapies which take only an hour or so to accomplish usually have very poor and short-lasting results. The steady and gradual changes explained in this book are designed to last for as long as you desire to use them. I want the reduction of phobias to become a part of your daily lifestyle.

The third assumption is:

PHOBIA REDUCTION COMES FROM PRACTICING

Fear reduction is an active process. While you could gain a good deal of insight into your phobias by reading this book, it will not relieve your phobias unless you actively follow through with the program. You must continually practice the concepts.

Years of planning and research have gone into this program so that you might achieve a good measure of success right from the beginning. While you may not understand the full reason for all the exercises, they are planned in a specific order, so please stick to the plan as presented and practice every single day. Of course, in the beginning this will require some effort. Later on, however, the time needed to practice will be minimal.

As a parting word, remember:

NO PRACTICE = NO CHANGE

Neal Olshan, Ph.D.

CHAPTER ONE
Everyone Has Phobias

"Taking a new step, uttering a new word, is what people fear most."
FËDOR DOSTOEVSKI

How often have you felt sick at the thought of getting on an airplane? Wished you didn't have to go to a party because you hate meeting new people? Sweated bullets at the idea of making a speech? Dreaded being fired from your job or hated the thought of looking for a new one?

Everyone has phobias or unfounded fears about things they may have to do almost every day of their lives. Children dread going to school. Adolescents worry about dating and flunking exams. Adults fear lack of money or rejection by someone they love.

Some of us have more specific fears, often based on experiences that have decreased our confidence, such as fear of water, animals, dentists, the dark or heights. For an estimated 10 million Americans, phobias have become a way of life. We take for granted our fears and obsessions and live in a state of heightened anxiety that is out of proportion to the demands of the situation.

Phobias are beyond voluntary control and cannot be explained or reasoned away. They can produce a host of harmful body reactions as well as avoidance of the object or situation we fear. The individual may realize that there is no real cause for fear but on entering the phobic situation panics completely.

For many years the phobic reaction has been misunderstood, misconstrued and mistreated. Many of us have a phobic reaction to something in our lives. When that reaction reaches a level of intensity that incapacitates us, then a method is needed to solve the problem. An inappropriate anxiety response may cause years of discomfort and trepidation if allowed to persist.

Whatever type of unfounded fear or phobia you suffer from, this book will explore the nature of such fears and provide help in overcoming them. For the longer a phobia exists, the more it disrupts our lives and the more it may actually lead to the occurrence of the thing we fear the most.

Howard Hughes, the elusive and eccentric multimillionaire, was a good example of this type of self-fulfilling prophecy. His obsession with privacy and secrecy probably stirred up more public interest in his affairs than a more normal but sheltered lifestyle would have done. Furthermore, his fanatical fear of doctors and hospitals led to kidney damage from abuse of non-prescription drugs, and eventually to his death, at a time when life-saving kidney transplants are almost as routine as gall bladder operations.

It is quite clear from numerous reports of his behavior that phobias controlled a good portion of Hughes' life. An immensely intricate web of fear reactions affected his ability to make rational decisions and live a normal life. Although extreme, his case is a perfect illustration of what can happen when a relatively minor fear is not resolved. Gradually it will grow into an immense web of phobic reactions. Whereas it once could have been resolved easily, the phobia becomes firmly engrained into the individual's pattern of behavior — the more he avoids the object of his phobia, the more he reinforces his fear.

ADMIT YOU HAVE FEARS

Admitting that you have uncontrollable fears is the first step in resolving them. People who insist that they are not afraid of anything are often fooling themselves or simply unaware that they are living a life that is less happy and fulfilling than it could be. Our bodies can be the source of a tremendous amount of energy, but fears and phobias can eat into it. Combine this with the energy needed to maintain an outwardly calm appearance and the phobic individual may be wasting ninety-five percent of his time.

Fears and phobias can touch every aspect of our lives at one time or another. They can affect how we function in business, in our social or sexual lives, and their haunting influence may determine how we develop relationships with other people.

Bob Jones was frantic. He had been trying for years without success to overcome his fear of airplanes. At first it had served him well as a joke. People were constantly chiding him about having to take boats, trains, and buses everywhere he went. His aversion to flying became so strong that even the thought of an airplane flight would cause severe nausea and dizziness. The sound of a plane flying overhead or just talking about his problem would make his hands tremble and his knees weak. "My knees feel as though they are made of water and if I don't sit down immediately I think I'm going to fall," he reported the first time he came to the treatment center.

This is no doddering seventy-year-old man speaking, but a screen actor in his early forties who has made numerous motion pictures. His public image is one of strength, virility and courage and many of his roles have involved actions that require great daring. Therein lies his bind. He needs to maintain a "macho" image, but his fear of flying has become so strong he can no longer hide behind the thin guise of a nonchalant distrust of airplanes.

His own words explain the situation best: "It's beginning to affect everything I do. Producers and sponsors wouldn't back a show if they realized how much flying bothered me. I feel like an old lady. Luckily, the last time I flew I was in first class and spent most of the trip in the bathroom, hugging the toilet. My wife kids me about the problem but not even she knows how bad it really is, because she likes to take cruises. So any time we go on a vacation we take a boat. But I can't go on this way. It's got to stop. I'm supposed to fly to Europe next month to begin shooting a new film, and every time I think about it my stomach does flip-flops."

Bob was faced with the traumatic effect of a phobia towards flying. His physical and emotional responses to that fear were way out of proportion to the real danger involved. Not all cases are as severe. Some people develop only minor symptoms as a result of a phobia towards flying. Others have even stronger reactions.

What can they do?

The movie star underwent therapy to resolve his flying phobia — not psychotherapy or analysis stretched out over several years to gain insight into the emotional cause of the problem. He didn't have time for that. Instead, he followed the fear reduction program involving a combination of self-induced relaxation and desensitization, which we will explain in detail later on.

Bob's problem was resolved within a month and he is now working on a film with several scenes in which he has to spend a considerable amount of time in a helicopter and on an airplane.

PHYSICAL SIGNS OF PHOBIA

The fear of flying shares one basic characteristic with all other phobias. The individual tries to avoid the object of his fear or anxiety in any manner possible, and when confronted with that object or situation displays a whole gamut of uncontrollable physical and emotional responses. Some of these responses may be so subtle as to be undetectable by the individual, such as slight perspiration or an uneasy feeling at the pit of the stomach, minor muscle weakness and changes in facial expression. Others are painfully obvious and may eventually incapacitate the person.

Some phobias, less easy to recognize than fear of flying, may trigger very severe reactions before the person becomes completely aware of what is happening to him or her.

Betty Harris was a 48-year-old widow who sold real estate. Her 24-year-old daughter was married and lived on the other side of town.

"I was very successful," Betty told me on her first visit, "and making sales on a weekly basis." But as she continued to relate the events that had taken place three years before, her voice started to waver.

"The morning had gone well and I was heading home for lunch. Suddenly at one of the stop lights my hands started to tremble. At first I thought it might be fatigue and that I was working too hard and too long. But the shaking got worse and began to travel up my arms. By the time I drove up the street to my house I could barely control the car.

"I went from doctor to doctor, but none of them could find anything physically wrong. Then I found that the only way to calm my nerves was to take a shot of bourbon several times a day. Never enough to let anyone know I'd been drinking, but it seemed to be the only thing that would stop the shaking."

"Did the shaking occur only while you were driving?" I asked. Betty answered, her voice filled with emotion, "Yes, in the beginning. Then it began to affect me when I worked with clients. I used to love meeting new people and suddenly I was afraid. Afraid to go into a house, afraid to meet new clients, and even afraid to get up in the morning."

"Did you ever undergo therapy at that time?"

"I had weekly sessions with a psychiatrist for two years, but I could only stop the shaking by taking a lot of medication and that made me want to go back to bed. I haven't worked in six months and if I don't find an answer soon, I'll lose my job."

Betty's case involved more than one specific phobia. Xenophobia — the fear of strangers — had been underlying her behavior for a long time. Only when the physical symptoms became severe did she realize how strongly her phobia affected her.

Unresolved and lying just below the surface, it festered and grew worse each day. Doctors could identify the symptoms but not treat them.

This patient underwent therapy at our center for one and a half months. During that time she received autogenic training, hypnosis and a desensitization program in which she learned to visualize the situations that caused her fear. She did much of the work on her own at home. Betty has now returned to work and at latest report is regaining her confidence and self-esteem. She is no longer fearful of unpredictable phobic attacks, because she is aware of her fears and has a tool to short-circuit the phobic reaction. Through constant practice, this woman can be confident that she will not be bothered with the same reactions in the future.

FEARS IN WOMEN

Fear of speaking before a group and agoraphobia — a multiple complex of fears involving leaving the house, traveling in planes, subways, buses, ships, and fear of closed spaces, such as elevators — are two of the most common phobias in women.

Fear of making speeches commonly affects young, seemingly independent and ambitious young women,[*] many of them struggling to enter occupational areas formerly dominated by men. Their phobia usually takes the form of a panic attack prior to a major presentation, such as a lecture, court date or radio broadcast. Most of the time, these young women are able to force themselves to perform, but unless they seek help they live in constant fear of similar attacks in the future.

At first, it would seem that fear of evaluation is the core of the problem — what others think, how they will be judged, as well as fear of negative evaluation or attack. However, another basic issue appears to be the fear of being out there alone with no one to depend on. For example, a young lawyer came in very anxious

[*]Information reprinted by permission of Dr. Iris Fodor, associate professor of educational psychology, New York University and BMA Audio Cassettes, New York.

and upset after her first court experience because the judge was not "taking care of her" in court. There is also the feeling that one has to be cool and cannot show anxiety under pressure. The problem is often aggravated if the young woman is the only female in the office in her type of job. The anxiety over loss of control of feelings becomes the focus of her phobia.

The fear of being alone is the basic fear experienced by the agoraphobic, who tends to be a young, married woman, living out the traditonal female role. The phobia and its accompanying anxieties often leave the woman feeling super-helpless and dependent. One woman, aged 41, was chronically anxious and feared death or sudden illness if she went out of the house. She had this problem on the street, on trains, in cars, going to the theater or to church. She had reached the point at which she could not perform any of her duties and was helpless. Her husband had to remain home with her and even then she continued to be frightened. This is an extreme case. Most agoraphobics can go out of the house and do almost anything in the company of their husbands or some other close relative or friend. But when forced to do things alone, they collapse.

Generally, agoraphobia involves two fears: the fear of being in the street or traveling alone, and the fear of having the anxiety or panic attack. The latter is often the most intense fear. Often, there is also an inability to put up with the nausea and dizziness that accompany fear.

Almost all agoraphobics are married, and their phobia usually strikes at about age 25, typically some five years after marriage. Usually the first attack occurs at a time of stress. In one case, the anxiety attack occurred in a young woman on the subway ride home from her psychoanalyst, when she brought up her wish to leave her husband. In another similar case, a young college student living at home began her subway phobia when her parents were away on a trip, and she was enjoying her first experience of freedom. She was waiting for a train to take her to the airport to meet her parents, worrying about whether she would make it on time, when her phobia began. In both cases, the phobia intensified the dependency of the woman on the family and spread so that neither was able to travel alone.

Most women who develop either agoraphobia or performance anxiety have personalities which show dependence and avoidance. Their parents were often overprotective, creating dependency in the daughter, and their avoidance shows itself in two ways:

1. A tendency to avoid assertion, particularly of angry feelings.
2. To avoid learning how to cope with feared situations, or mastering situations which would foster the development of confidence.

Women with anxiety about speaking in public vary from being super cool and independent to girlish and immature. What is common to most cases is that of being the older of two daughters and of being singled out as special for achievement. The family holds up perfectionistic standards and the daughters are criticized when they fail to achieve this standard. They are also taught to hide feelings, often by keeping a "stiff upper lip."

Most of the mothers of such women often lived out the conventional mother role and were generally looked down on by their daughters. Although the mothers are highly critical of their daughters, they are seen as being incapable of doing much themselves. The fathers were often critical of the mother's behavior. So the daughter grew up with a strong feeling of not wanting to be like Mother.

Under stress, or while experiencing the anxiety of the phobia, there is a fear that they are behaving exactly like their mothers — helpless, dependent, hysterical and incompetent.

Thus, for both types of phobias, the experience is one of super-helplessness, avoidance of mastering their fears and anticipating anxiety when forced to face the subject of their fear.

Nancy was in her mid-forties. Her husband was a doctor and made a good living. Since both children were away at college she had little to occupy her at home and became deeply involved in charitable work. Each morning, after preparing her husband's breakfast, she would set out for the hospital where she worked on various committees. Gradually, Nancy was elected to more and more responsible positions until finally she was asked to chair the hospital's fund-raising committee. This required a considerable amount of contact with hospital administrators, other doctors' wives and people from the community.

At first, Nancy handled the responsibilities admirably, making speeches, holding luncheons and constantly meeting new people in her efforts to raise money for the hospital. But gradually the pressures of the work began to get to her and she would occasionally hear criticism of her performance from less prominent, and probably jealous committee members. She began to get less and less pleasure out of her efforts and became increasingly frightened at speaking in front of groups. Small problems, that previously she had handled without an effort, began to make her frustrated and angry, and the anger would hang on for many minutes after an incident.

Her behavior was changing from that of a competent, self-assured woman, who enjoyed what she was doing, to one who was frightened of criticism and too perfectionistic to be secure. She started avoiding her friends, walking up stairs, instead of taking the elevator and fleeing if a group of people approached. Nancy's complete avoidance of meeting people reached a peak when she refused to go to dinner with one of her husband's new colleagues.

In her attempts to break out of her former role as a housewife and mother she had become increasingly self-demanding, and had tried to go too far, too fast. The slightest criticism of her work would upset her enormously until she became incapacitated by fear of failure.

Week by week she became more and more reclusive and seldom ventured out of the house. Finally, in desperation, her husband contacted me and sought my advice. I suggested that his wife try the fear reduction program. At this point, it is important to note that unless someone is willing to try to reduce their phobia, forcing them to do so will lead to extremely poor results, and in many cases will have an adverse effect.

Commitment by the individual to the self-help program is essential.

Nancy went through the fear reduction program and found that her level of fearfulness and anxiety dropped considerably. There was some residual anxiety and she had to repeat some parts of the program. The second time around, a further phobic reaction towards meeting new people was identified. This secondary phobic reaction was not as intense as her fear of failure, but came into prominence when the initial phobic reaction was terminated. Since Nancy had by this time become adept at the fear reduction program, it was a simple matter for her to reduce this secondary fear and she was soon free to resume her fund-raising activities.

Phobic reactions towards those of the opposite sex (genophobia) are also common. In fact, this phobia is experienced to some degree by approximately 63 percent of men and women. Most people experience this phobia in a mild form in adolescence. The pressures and expectations of young people with regard to dating may cause genophobia to surface.

The young person who does not adequately resolve this phobia may carry it with him into later relationships which may affect him on a job, during social gatherings or in a marital relationship.

Ray was such a young man, referred to me by his family doctor. The boy had gone in for a regular checkup and, while discussing sports with the doctor, had mentioned that whenever he was around girls, his palms became sweaty, he got butterflies in his stomach and felt just like he did before the start of a football game. Ray had no physical problems and as a sophomore in high school, at over six feet tall, and 180 pounds, he was extremely popular, besides being a good student and active in extracurricular activities.

As he described the situation with girls further, the doctor became aware that this was not a normal anxiety response to going out on dates. He questioned the boy at length and found out that Ray had dated on only one occasion. Afterwards he felt so anxious and physically upset that he had avoided any contact with girls. He had successfully hidden his fear from his friends, and even his parents were not aware of the situation. He simply excused himself on the grounds that he had to practice sports or was too busy with his studies.

Over the phone, I questioned the doctor further and found out that Ray was an only child. He was very attached to his mother and had not spent a great deal of time in activities with his father, who was a salesman and traveled a great deal.

I felt that since Ray had become so attached to his mother, dating girls may have made him feel she would be angry at him for displaying interest in another female. The fear that he would "make a fool out of himself" also played a part.

Ray's doctor shared my concern that if this phobia was not resolved now, it would cause severe difficulties later on. Since it is my feeling that dating is a natural and necessary part of one's social development, I agreed to provide Ray with the fear reduction program. He dropped by my office one afternoon and I spent a brief time going over it with him. I stressed that his parents should be aware of the situation and was told that they already knew Ray was coming to see me about getting over his fear of dating. He did not want to go into any more detail about it with them and I assured him that he could initiate and practice the program by himself, if he was committed to solving the problem.

At first he was somewhat hesitant and I pointed out that this method of reducing his phobia towards girls would only work if he really and truly wanted to lose the fear. He reassured me that this was so and that in fact he had a crush on a girl who was in his English class, but up until this time had been too scared to ask her out. There was a big dance after the last football game in a month's time and he hoped to resolve his problem by then so that he could ask her out.

Ray took the program home and I also supplied him with one of the relaxation-autogenic training tapes to be played in his cassette recorder. These tapes can be made by anyone following the script provided in Chapters 5 – 6 of this book. Ray called me on several occasions with questions concerning his progress. Mostly he simply wanted to be reassured that he was doing well in his therapy. The next time I heard from him, he had asked the girl out on a date and was preparing for the dance.

He was sure the program would prevent him from feeling scared while on the date because he had practiced the technique to overcome his fears before football games and found he was much more relaxed. In fact, since he was less anxious his performance had improved considerably.

He reassured himself by repeating "I tried it and it really works. It really works and I know I'm going to have a good time."

Once a phobia has been identified and acknowledged, then treatment can be presented and applied to combat it. Phobias cannot be ignored or wished away. Sound scientific methods are needed to help people reduce anxiety and, whenever possible, to eliminate their phobias.

"In terms of our personal growth, we cannot move on until we are attentive to the present moment. There is no real 'moving on' to leave conflicts and unresolved situations behind. The anger, the fear, the frustration we have, stays with us unless it is expressed or satisfied in some way. It holds onto our energy and will subtly control us, popping up again and again, perhaps at different places, but it is the same old fear nevertheless.

Fear is that one emotion which dooms us to repeat our mistakes of the past. Because we have been hurt we will carry it with us, afraid to be hurt again, and live out the self-defeating patterns our fear of pain sets up — unless we take the wherewithal to face what it is we are afraid of.

We cannot change the past. We cannot truly deal with the future. The only moment we can give ourselves to is now. We cannot forget our fears; nor can we really predict, even in the next moment, what love or pain will come to us. But we try. We hold onto old hurts and predict new ones, and fear, that mysterious, haunting, ever-present dark cloud, pervades our past, present and future time and waits to be embraced.''*

So, if we are to grow, we must focus our attention towards what is happening to us in the present. The resolution of unresolved fears cannot be left to chance. It is in our nature that fears which remain untreated will constantly be robbing us of energy, emotional and psychological growth, and the ability to enjoy life. A fear long forgotten is not a fear resolved. The ghosts of old fears constantly reappear to haunt us.

Unless we are prepared to deal with fear, we are destined to constantly repeat unproductive actions of the past. One day we experience a fear reaction, and it may stay with us throughout our lifetime. Whether this fear reaction occurred yesterday or 25 years ago, it still exerts its influence to keep us in a vicious cycle of self-defeating, non-assertive behaviors.

Fears have been with us since the beginning of time and will persist through eternity. Fear is the wild animal that can never be completely tamed, but we can do our best to cage it, learn more from it, and gain control over its behavior.

Only you can take the first step to identify and overcome your fears.

*John T. Wood, ''What Are You Afraid Of?'' *A Guide to Dealing With Your Fears* (Englewood Cliffs, N.J.: Spectrum Books, 1975), p. 34.

CHAPTER TWO
How We Develop Phobias

> *"I shall define phobia to be a fear of an imaginary evil, or an undue fear of a real one."*
>
> BENJAMIN RUSH, 1798

Fear has been defined as a reaction to a real danger, whereas anxiety and phobias are defined as reactions to a situation that may, in reality, not be dangerous or harmful. However, many times the difference between the two narrows down to a subjective evaluation.

Hebb (1940) has suggested that the essence of fear is brain disorganization, brought about by stimuli for which there is no adequate response. The responses which are generated are incompatible with the stimulus and cannot be smoothly completed. In this way, the brain's ability to process and respond to the stimulus becomes disorganized; energy is mobilized which cannot be appropriately discharged, and the result is the uncoordinated, helpless behavior we associate with fear.

Take, for example, Alex who was in a devasting automobile accident and saw his wife and young child killed. The scene was so painful, and his ability to respond to it so inadequate, that his brain blocked out the memory of the accident. All the information was stored away in his brain in a disorganized and unrelated fashion and then could not consciously be recalled. As a result of this frightening and tragic experience, Alex developed a pathologic fear of driving cars.

At the present time, many scientists share the belief that most fears are learned, and most phobias develop from unresolved fears.

The young child who is stung by a bee develops a fear of bees and as a result may avoid walking in the grass, avoid sniffing flowers and develop a distaste for honey. This is a perfect example of a major traumatic incident resulting in a learned fear response, which generalizes to other objects or situations.

An example of how a fear is learned from a previously neutral cue can be illustrated by numerous animal experiments in which a certain pleasurable experience, such as eating, is combined with an unpleasant electric shock. Gradually the animal learns to fear eating. A previously neutral cue (food) can now elicit a fear response. A fear has been learned.

Some people develop fears because they are exposed to faulty alternatives. All of us watch the people around us and receive information from them. When we are younger, our main models for behavior are parents, grandparents, and brothers or sisters. We also spend a great deal of time developing behaviors from observing kids who are older than we are. This learning-through-modeling process does not stop when we reach our teen years, but continues on through our adult life. When we see a parent express fear at getting on an airplane or a brother afraid to ride in a car, then we ourselves may learn to fear these things. Unfortunately we can become the victims of the people who are closest to us. After years of having parental models presenting their fears to us, it is very likely that we will develop the same reactions. From these learned reactions we can then go on to develop phobias. Although fears are not hereditary in a genetic sense, like the color of hair or eyes, they can be passed on from one generation to another as a result of parental behavior.

Bob, who was thirty-four years old, developed a fear of losing his job. Despite a college education, he constantly dreaded the day when his boss would fire him. His work performance suffered greatly as a result and brought about his dismissal on several occasions. Because he was in a constant state of uneasiness, he developed bad working habits. The fear which was reinforced by several firings, was now a full-blown phobia.

Reaching back into his history, he found that the fear started because his father had constantly come home and confided in the family his worry of losing a job. He remembered that his father had not been able to hold employment for any length of time and they were constantly moving because his father had to seek a new job. He even remembered his mother telling him that his grandfather had experienced the same problem. Through this defective modeling behavior, he was destined to develop a phobic reaction towards losing his job.

It is easy to see from the above example how defective modeling behavior can cause a phobic reaction. Modeling is not the only way in which we learn phobias. Sometimes the advice that people give us can cause a fear reaction. If we are constantly told as children not to ride in cars because they are dangerous, not to go up inside tall buildings, to be careful of all dogs, and to watch out for bugs because they are poisonous, we eventually learn to believe in some of these exaggerated fears. This is not to say that all such warnings are ill-advised. Someone who tells you not to stand under a tree during a thunderstorm is giving you very good and possibly lifesaving advice. It is therefore extremely important for the child to have an opportunity to process all modeling behavior and all advice — to sort it out for himself, and to retrieve the good advice while throwing away the bad.

Ask yourself what you're learning from others

FEARS MAY PERSIST BECAUSE OTHERS REINFORCE THEM
Any time you receive reinforcement for a thought or an act, there is an increased chance that the thought or act will be repeated in

the future. If you make a face and people laugh at you, there is a good chance that you will do this again in order to obtain the same result. The more often you receive a positive response, the more permanently engrained this act will become.

Many parents teach their children to be fearful by reinforcing certain behaviors. The mother who tells Betty not to go near any dogs because they may bite her, reinforces this fear by praising her daughter for not going near one. As the girl grows older, her fear of dogs may develop into a phobia which will stay with her throughout her lifetime because of the strong reinforcement from her mother.

We count on our parents to help reinforce some fears, such as staying away from poisonous snakes or loaded guns, but inadvertently many parents instill unreasonable fears in us through positive reinforcement of fearful behavior.

PHOBIAS MAY DEVELOP FROM IGNORANCE

Some irrational fears develop through ignorance. For example, millions of Americans are afraid of flying, and many of their fears are based on lack of knowledge of how an airplane operates. To counteract this, Pan Am holds periodic seminars on overcoming fear of flying, in large cities. The course consists primarily of lectures on aerodynamics plus a tour of the airport control tower and a brief flight, during which the various mechanical procedures and accompanying noises are explained.

Typical of the person who takes the Pan Am course was one woman who feared that when she stepped onto a plane the weight of her body would tip it over. Farfetched? Maybe. But true, and not unusual when you consider how irrational phobias can be.

Fear of elevators is another common phobia which can develop through ignorance. In New York, Dr. Manuel Zane, a former psychoanalyst who has turned to behavior therapy, took a group of nine of his patients, who were terrified of elevators, through an experience he designed just for them. He did not go through the usual relaxing exercises you will learn later, but took them to a downtown building where they were given a quick course on elevators. A representative of the Otis Elevator Company took the group on a tour of the workings of an elevator, above and below ground. Patients found out exactly what made it work and what could go wrong and what couldn't. Some of them were relieved when they learned that the elevator couldn't possibly lose control and crash through the roof.

During the "class" Zane's patients were constantly monitoring and talking about their fear levels. He even had them assign ratings, from 1 to 10, to the things they were afraid of. They talked amongst themselves, to the man from Otis, and to Zane, about the things that were right in front of them — the elevator buttons, the doors, the hatch at the top. At the end of a ten-week session, each of the nine people involved in the program was riding in the elevator alone.

A CASE OF FEAR DEVELOPMENT

As we have already seen, a bad accident can lead to the development of a phobia, and in some cases may severely disrupt a person's life.

When Captain James Morrison was involved in a severe plane crash during WW II, it was very easy to see why he was fearful of flying. A long hospitalization after the crash and years of rehabilitation had firmly implanted a severe phobia towards flying. In this case, the fear of planes generalized to a phobia of hearing planes overhead, seeing pictures of planes, talking about flying and even seeing small models of airplanes. These cues now evoked the same types of response as if he were actually sitting in an airplane. Usually such secondary phobias do not elicit as severe a fear reaction as the primary phobia. But, if these secondary phobias are combined, the fear reaction may actually be as great, if not slightly greater, than the initial fear response, since secondary phobias tend to have a cumulative effect.

Morrison found that when he stopped thinking or talking about airplanes, he became less tense. If a picture of an airplane came on television, he would quickly look away. While in a business meeting, the discussion turned to reviewing a trip by one of his subordinates. During the discussion, the employee began to talk about his airplane flight. Morrison immediately stood up and excused himself from the room. He did not return until the discussion of the airplane flight was over.

By stopping his thoughts about airplanes, he reduced his fear response but reinforced the avoidance of the feared situation. His behavior then became obsessional, to avoid any contact with, mention of, or thoughts about flying on airplanes.

The above case is very easily understood, but not all fear responses follow this typical pattern. Many times, a person has to search for the roots of his or her fear reaction.

In women, some psychologists, including Dr. Iris Fodor of New York University, believe that socialization into traditional female roles courts the development of phobias. For example, when mental health professionals were asked to rate traits of a healthy woman, in contrast to those of a healthy man, they reported a healthy woman as being: emotional, submissive, excitable, passive, house-oriented, not at all adventurous, and showing a strong need for security and dependency. In contrast, the stereotypic male role stressed strength, mastery, coolness, keeping feelings under control, competence, bravery, assertiveness. These desirable traits for men are the exact opposite of the phobic state.

All children start off helpless and dependent, but the research of Hoffman, and others, suggests that girls continue to be reinforced for this dependency and boys for autonomy. Similarly, while boys and girls both start off equally fearful as children, studies of adolescents report that 20% of girls are still fearful. Childhood experience teaches and reinforces these stereotypes. The mass media presents super-exaggerated versions of stereotypic male and female roles via television, films and books. Small wonder that parents have little influence in changing the traditional stereotype. Thus, boys and girls, who are not too different from one another to begin with, are repeatedly exposed to the view that boys and men are brave and hide vulnerable feelings, while girls are passive, dependent, submissive, fearful and incompetent.

In a NOW task force study entitled "Dick and Jane as victims," conducted on 134 elementary school reading books nationally, the following was found: When one examines the pictures, boys are shown doing brave, adventurous, even superhuman feats, such as riding alligators and shooting buffaloes, while girls are most often behind fences, or windows, immobilized, waiting. In pictures, the girls already appear to have agoraphobia. The dialogue parallels the pictures. The following are excerpts from children's reading books: "Look at her mother. Just look at her. She's just a girl. She gives up . . ." "Helplessness swept over her like a sickening wave. I can't, I can't, Amy was crying. It won't push. Oh Stuey, get me out. It's so dark in here . . ." "He felt a tear coming into his eye. But he brushed it away with his hands. Boys eight years old don't cry . . ." "Cries of fright came from the woman and children around her . . ." "Oh Raymond, boys are so much braver than girls . . ." "Roger's mother wept, afraid that her son would be eaten. But Roger was a brave boy . . ." "Sam led and Helen went after him. Helen held his hand in a hard grip. She was timid in the darkness. Helen fell and Sam helped her get up."

The sex role socialization message is clear.

Boys are taught to be brave and master their fears and incompetencies. Girls are presented with fearful dependent role models who lean on males. Few competent female models are presented. Thus, under stress, succumbing to the traditional role may be a natural route and the sex role message gets translated into male and female coping styles. Phobias may be viewed in this way as a natural outcome of sex role socialization, rather than an illness.

Performance anxieties or fear of speaking in front of a group can be understood in this context as follows:

The young woman, trying to be competent and having few positive shaping experiences for her burgeoning attempts at mastery, tries to adapt the male coping style of coolness under stress, and experiences the normal anxiety common to the situation. Since she had been led to believe that coolness is expected, she becomes anxious about her anxious feelings, which may set off the very response she is most fearful of — behaving like a hysterical female. In some sense, both performance anxiety and agoraphobia can be seen as solutions to the adolescent struggles over dependency and independency. Phobias seem to arise in young adults when an apprehensive, dependent, immature person is trying to realize his or her ambitions and become an independent, successful member of society.

For some young women, the adolescent struggle is a time to choose between the positive traits considered desirable for men and adults and have their femininity questioned, or to behave in the prescribed feminine manner and accept second-class adult status. The performance-anxious young women are trying the less traditional role and are trying to forge their own way along an uncertain route, while the agoraphobics choose the traditional route to independence — marriage.

How does uncertainty about these choices contribute to the development of phobias? For performance-anxious young women, and the same might be true for many young men in this category, it is the step into the limelight that is the focus of the anxiety. Often one sees a form of a fear of success — a disposition to become anxious about achieving success, because they expect negative consequences, such as social rejection, and/or a feeling of being unfeminine, as a result of succeeding. Further, these young women have had lots of don'ts, but they have had little positive reinforcement history to guide them for this type of mastery, and even fewer models in their families, and society in general, to copy. Hence, the anxiety about how to behave, doubts about whether they will or can succeed, worry about the audience, as well as fear about the effects of success seem reasonable. Too often, in fact, the men respond to the tears and shore the weeping women up. But competent women do, too often, have to stand alone, says Dr. Fodor.

WOMEN'S ROLES AND AGORAPHOBIA

Agoraphobia can also be viewed as an outcome of the adolescent struggle. It usually occurs in women choosing the more traditional role. There is nothing in the media to prepare women for the adult, female role — a woman who could be more than a wife and mother. The media emphasizes the romantic nature of marriage and motherhood, but does not prepare women for the realistic responsibilities of marriage, or train them in establishing and maintaining autonomy within a relationship. Agoraphobic women tend to come from overprotective families. They appear to marry dominating men and somewhere, early in the marriage, handle the realistic stress of marriage or children by slipping into the exaggeration of a stereotypic role. Occasionally, one sees agoraphobic young women still living at home with their parents, or still caught up with the adolescent separation from home.

What happens when a young woman, who is apparently independent, self-sufficient and capable, changes after marriage and develops phobias or other signs of constriction of self? These changes invariably cause her to become excessively dependent and helpless. She becomes fearful of travel, to be alone even for a moment; she usually can no longer drive a car herself. In less dramatic cases, she becomes fearful of making decisions or of taking any responsibilities of her own. She clings to her husband for constant support, apparently changing from a capable, strong person into the classically helpless female.

Wolpe, a leading behavior therapist, in discussing three agoraphobic women, makes a similar point. A kind of trapped feeling is being experienced by the patients. A very large percentage of the patients are female and married and the feelings develop concurrently with feelings of wanting to break or violate the strictures of the marriage contract. It is essential to establish the emotional freedom needed to leave the marriage before being able to overcome the agoraphobic symptoms. Thus, we see that agoraphobia may be related to feelings of trappedness, with no outlet for assertion, or making one's own way. The consequence of making a move out becomes dangerous, anxiety-provoking. And the phobia, in some sense, comes out on the side of the dependency, as it leaves the woman more helpless, dependent and submissive.

Women can't flee if they fear flying, as Erica Jong made clear. Agoraphobia may also allow for some expression of anger, even indirectly, since it prevents the husband from taking trips, too, and demands of him extra sacrifices. The struggle in the marriage is often a re-enactment of the childhood separation experiences, with the spouse taking the place of the parent. However, it is different, because men presumably struggle with their masculine stereotypic image, which often makes them strong and brave, in contrast to the helpless, incompetent woman — an image society constantly reinforces. A woman's struggle for autonomy in marriage may threaten the husband's own sexual identity struggle. Furthermore, while in the early separation from the parents there was a marriage to escape to. This time, like Ibsen's Nora, the possibility of looking into a void is frightening. For women, unhappy in this type of marriage, fantasies of a romantic escape with another man may prevent a phobia. In other women, this trappedness may lead to phobia. The conflict can be understood as follows:

1. Women may fear being autonomous and independent but wish for the same as well.

2. There is a thread of loss of external reinforcement, either in the form of loss of love of the husband, of the parent or of economic support.

3. The suppressed, independent, assertive strivings represent temptation. Women have been conditioned to feel guilty if they deviate from the stereotypic role, and exhibit behavior which has been labeled unfeminine.

4. Avoidant responses have been the major way of handling conflict. There is a symbolic association between the feared stimulus and suppressed striving. They can represent the wish to flee — e.g. fear of trains, or avoidance of situations that

remind one of current trappedness, e.g. claustrophobia, fear of elevators and enclosures. Or there can be avoidance at succeeding in what is perceived as the male role, as in women with perform-ance anxieties.

5. By being phobic, the woman avoids the independent adult role and becomes dependent and childlike again. There is an interper-sonal message that says: I am a distressed, weak, unhappy person in need of your help and direction. The family and husband reinforce this dependency, since they may prefer her to be phobic and tied to them rather than free, independent and well.

Thus, the issue for phobic women is to resolve the conflict between their dependent and independent strivings, and to help break the familial and societal patterns that maintain the phobia. Fear reduction techniques which you will learn in this book, may be viewed as providing the new learning experience that is a powerful antidote to the parental and societal sex-role program-ming that all woman are exposed to, and phobics apparently succumb to.

Prior to the late 1950's, most agoraphobic patients were treated by various forms of psychotherapy, including Freudian psycho-analysis. In the late 1950's, Drs. Wolpe and Rachman began treating this type of patient with the behavior modification tech-nique known as systematic desensitization.

During the middle and late 60's, research into the treatment of agoraphobic patients showed that desensitization appeared to be a superior method to individual or group psychotherapy. These controlled studies also showed that no significant symptom sub-stitution was present. In other words, systematic desensitization was an excellent therapy for agoraphobia and once the individual was able to control the fear, no new symptoms took its place. A study in 1968 by Gelder & Marks, showed that seven patients previously treated in group psychotherapy for two years, with no discernable improvement, showed great improvement when they used the desensitization process for four months. I have read of several recent studies which have attempted to make a comparison of: psychotherapy, behavior therapy, relaxation and desensitization, relaxation alone, and desensitization alone. The data reported so far seem to indicate that the process of relaxation combined with desensitization has a better overall success rate.

Since many of the symptoms of agoraphobia are not directed towards a specific stimulus, the identification of this phobia may be somewhat difficult. The patient feels many different symptoms and therefore, without an instrument such as the fear identification inventory I will present in Chapter 4, it is very difficult for her to identify the exact source of her discomfort. Unfortunately, many professionals in the past would "dump" patients into the agoraphobic category without adequately investigating the possibility of specific phobias. This term became a catch-all phrase during the early 1950's. Even today, some mental health professionals continue to use the term to describe situations which do not lend themselves to the overall category of agoraphobia.

Repressed sexual desires, for example, can contribute to the development of phobias, and may be totally overlooked. One young woman developed a fear of crowded subway trains because of a secret wish for a sexual encounter in the traffic and excitement of the rush hour.

FEAR OF THE FUTURE
Fear of what may lie ahead in the future is another way in which genuine maladaptive phobic behaviors can develop. Since no one can predict the future, people who sit and worry that something drastic is going to happen to them may waste away their lives worrying about the next day and then the next day after that. Seldom, if ever, does reality live up to our fears about the future.

Such statements as:

"I just know I'm going to fail the test tomorrow"; "I know I'll be scared"; "I'm sure he won't like me"; "What if . . . ?"; "I just know that's going to hurt"; or "I know I can't do it, even if I try" are typical of the statements made by people who fear the future.

The "I just know it will happen," and the "What if" syndromes are very significant factors in the development of fears. No one is able to foretell the future and by fearing what may lie ahead, one automatically sets oneself up for developing a phobia. These fears can spread and in a short time you can find yourself fearful of many things in the future, most of them never happening. Nonetheless you develop all the physical and psychological symptoms of a severe phobic reaction.

You should keep reminding yourself that some fear is a natural ingredient of life experience. During war time situations, pilots and infantrymen reported that a certain amount of fear helped them perform their functions. This may be directly tied to the self-preservation or survival instinct. When these fears begin to control a person's life and develop in an irrational manner, however, they then become phobias.

Fritz Perls, originator of Gestalt therapy, did a considerable amount of theorizing on the basic premise of fear.

"If we don't know whether we will get applause or tomatoes, we hesitate; the heart begins to race; all our excitement can't flow into activity, and we develop stage fright. So the formula for anxiety is very simple: the gap between the now and the then."

Perls' reference to anticipating tomatoes instead of applause follows the premise of anticipating bad fortune before it actually happens. There seems to be a preoccupation with dwelling on the possibility that the future may hold failure and fearful situations. As Perls states: "The gap between the now and the then creates a feeling of anxiety, which leads to fear and in turn creates a phobic reaction."

The following short exercise will help you better realize what fears a gap between the "now" and the "then" may hold for you.

FUTURE FEAR

In the next few minutes, list three situations pertaining to a fear of something which may happen in the future. Try to limit the situations to future fearful events, not ones which have already happened. If you have always been fearful of boats and often have to take voyages, then do not use this as an example. But if you are fearful of swimming in the ocean and have never experienced that situation, then use that in the exercise you are about to complete. Remember, your phobia develops from the gap between what is happening at this moment and what you think will happen in the future.

Example:
A. *What you think the future fear will be:*
   Riding in a small, fast sports car.

B. *The catastrophic event you're sure will happen:*
   The car will be going very fast and the driver will probably be reckless which will cause an accident.

1. A. *What you think the future fear will be:*
   B. The catastrophic event you're sure will happen:

2. A. *What you think the future fear will be:*
   B. The catastrophic event you're sure will happen:

3. A. *What you think the future fear will be:*
   B. The catastrophic event you're sure will happen:

Now take a look at the three situations which you have listed in the exercise. No one can foretell the future, but there is a good chance that many of your catastrophic fantasies will never come true. If you think about them continuously, then the chances of the feared event actually happening may increase. Exaggerating the possibility of an unhappy outcome may only lead to the feared event itself.

HOW DO WE MAINTAIN FEAR?
We have pointed out that animals can be made to show a fear response by taking a previously neutral response cue (stimulus) and pairing it with another stimulus which already produces a fear response. Since we may consider pain as an innate producer of fear, a neutral stimulus combined with a pain stimulus may produce fear.

Pain, disfigurement, uncomfortable body sensations exclusive of pain, and mental anguish may be reinforcers of basic fear responses.

Since fear can be learned so quickly, and manifests itself in such a strong manner, many behavioral scientists, including Freud, feel that uncontrolled fear and unresolved severe anxiety may lead to conflicts which eventually develop into neurotic behavior. The person who has many fears and phobias, and makes no attempt to resolve them, will spend a great deal of time denying and trying to avoid the fear-producing stimulus. Little does he realize that the fear stimulus may be causing the phobias to spread to other areas of his personality. His obsession with avoiding the fearful stimulus and his multiple phobias may cause a severe amount of physical and emotional discomfort.

Sleep phobia is particularly debilitating and usually the patient runs a complete course of drugs and medications before coming to the realization that his or her aversion to sleep may not have an organic basis.

People may develop chronic phobic reactions to sleep for many different reasons. One of the most common explanations for this type of reaction in older patients is the fear of going to sleep and dying during the night. This fear may have developed out of a prolonged illness and the sudden realization that life will not go on forever. If a close friend or acquaintance has died recently, the reality of death itself may cause the older individual to develop the phobic reaction towards sleep. This fear of sleep is constantly reinforced by news reports of people who die in their sleep, either from natural causes or as the result of disease.

A second form of sleep phobia may develop out of early behaviors as a child. If, as a youngster, an individual is scared during the night or suffers from extreme nightmares, then he or she will develop an avoidance reaction and fear going to sleep. Sleeplessness soon becomes a habit and he is caught in the buildup of a chronic phobic reaction. The more he tries to avoid sleep, the more fatigued he becomes. Such people commonly will fight sleep into the wee hours of the night and, finally exhausted, drop into a very fitful and restless sleep at 4 or 5 in the morning. The alarm clock shatters their fitful sleep and in many ways relieves them of the trauma induced by the fear of sleep. Relief from this fear is only short-lived as they again begin to prepare themselves for the next evening. Phobic thoughts may permeate their entire day as their level of anxiety increases steadily, hour by hour.

The third way in which this phobia can develop is through traumatic incidents happening later in life. The following case history will illustrate the development of a phobic reaction towards sleep in a 28-year-old male.

For years Roger had not been a good sleeper. Tossing and turning became routine during his sleeping hours. Most of the time he would stay up late at night, in an attempt to fatigue himself into a deeper sleep. By one or two in the morning he was completely exhausted and would fall into a fitful, shallow sleep. By 5:30 in the morning, he was up and ready to start another day of work as a construction supervisor for a large local construction firm.

This lack of consistent sleep led to a very erratic work record. By Thursday or Friday, he would be so exhausted that his employer would begin to notice that he was not performing his job adequately. He spent weekends in a medication-induced sleep, trying to regain lost sleep time.

The lack of sleep was not only affecting his job, but was changing his personality. He had become very short-tempered with people and had a very low tolerance for frustration. Depression slowly set in and many of his friends commented that he was becoming difficult to spend time with. His frustration turned to anger as, one by one, his friendships began to dissolve.

Roger's first statement to me typifies the pleading of many patients for some resolution to their problem, other than medication. In most cases, medication for sleep problems only works for a short period of time and then as the body adapts to the medication, the dosage has to be increased. This increased dosage gradually causes detrimental effects which impair psychological and emotional functioning.

I saw Roger for two sessions and checked into his prior medical history. All his physicians agreed that there was no organic reason for his inability to sleep and several of them had labeled him a neurotic. In my opinion, he *was* displaying neurotic behavior, in his inability to sleep, but he did not display any tendency towards severe emotional problems.

Roger was able to describe his fear reaction in the minutest detail.

"It all starts around four in the afternoon," he said.

"Tell me exactly what starts at four in the afternoon," I said, hoping to define his reaction more precisely.

Roger started immediately: "I'm tired and I start thinking about the night and how I'm not going to be able to sleep." He hesitated, but went on. "I get this strange feeling that I'm going to start shaking all over. I leave my job around four-thirty and on the way home all I can think about is how nice it would be to fall into a bed and sleep, and sleep and sleep."

"What do you do when you get home?"

"I usually stop at the store on the way home . . . I'm a bachelor . . . and pick up something for dinner. I'm not one to eat out. After dinner, I sit down, usually with a couple of beers, and watch television."

"Your mind is only on watching television?"

"I wish it was. No matter which program I'm watching, I always start thinking about sleep."

I pressed further. "Do your feelings of shakiness and uneasiness increase as the evening progresses?"

"They sure do!"

"Tell me about them."

Roger went on to describe how the shaking of his limbs would begin to increase as the evening progressed. The light disturbance in his stomach would become so aggravating that he would actually think he was going to throw up.

I asked him if he ever did throw up and he said that on occasion he had come pretty close. As the evening progresses, he is able to concentrate less and less on the television programs and they do not serve the purpose of distracting him at all. He reported to me that a previous doctor had prescribed Elavil, an antidepressant drug, and all this drug did was to make him more nervous and jittery.

By the time the news comes on at 11 P.M., Roger is in a state of severe anxiety and increasing depression. He is becoming more anxious and fearful as the normal sleep time approaches and also becoming increasingly depressed with the thought of not being able to go to sleep. I asked Roger when he first noticed this problem about getting to sleep.

"It was just after my father died five years ago," Roger said with some emotion in his voice.

"Were you very close to your father?"

"Very."

I probed further. "How did your father die?"

He hesitated for a moment. "In bed."

"Was he sick or did he have a stroke, something of that sort?"

"No, nothing like that. He had been healthy all his life and never spent more than a half a day being sick, no matter what it was. I always remember him as being the healthiest man I have ever known."

"What happened to change that?" I asked.

"Nothing! He just went to bed one night and died in his sleep. Fifty-six years old and he just died in his sleep. The doctor said it was natural causes — his body just stopped functioning."

I now had the reason for this individual's extreme fear of going to sleep. After a short discussion with him, he concurred that since his father's death, he had an overwhelming fear that he, too, would go to sleep one night and not awaken.

This fear had become so powerful that it affected both his conscious and subconscious thinking. It was as if he had been given a hypnotic suggestion that he would not go to sleep and if he did fall asleep for any length of time, he would surely die. Roger went through the relaxation and desensitization program, which we will describe in detail in Chapters 5 and 6.

Gradually he became less fearful of falling asleep and at the same time his fear of *not* falling asleep was being resolved.

I talked with Roger two months after he had begun his home therapy program and he reported that he was getting six to seven hours sleep each night and found that quite satisfactory. He was no longer waking up in the middle of the night with cold sweats and his job performance had improved greatly. The new-found energy gave him a better chance to enjoy life and influenced his future plans to the point where he had begun dating and was contemplating marriage.

I cautioned Roger that he might have to practice this therapy at spaced intervals for the next couple of years and he assured me that would be no problem and that he found the therapy basically enjoyable, anyway. As with most patients I have had the privilege of working with, Roger then began to use the phobia reduction program to influence other minor phobias and in this way improved other portions of his behavior.

Because it is obvious, as seen in the previous example, that fear is a conditioned or learned response, the "un-learning" can be helped considerably by using certain physical factors which inhibit it.

M. C. Jones, in a famous experiment of 1924, eliminated a child's fear of furry animals through the use of a rabbit and the pleasurable response of eating. All previous attempts at getting the child to touch the rabbit had failed. No amount of coercing or bribing with candy seemed to help. But because the child enjoyed eating, he allowed the rabbit to be gradually brought closer as he was eating. Slowly, but surely, the rabbit kept getting closer and closer, until finally the child was able to reach out and touch the rabbit with one hand.

The example illustrates two points: (1) that when a fear producing stimulus is combined with a pleasurable or relaxing stimulus, the phobic response may be lessened; (2) that the gradual manner in which the rabbit was brought forward helped the child to constantly adjust to the new situation. If the rabbit had suddenly been brought very close to the child, there is a good possibility that the fear response evoked by the rabbit would have been too sudden and strong to have been overridden by the pleasurable response of eating.

In dealing further with children, Watson and Rayner (1920), found that it was much harder to elicit a fear response from a child while he was sucking his thumb. Evidently the act of sucking the thumb was extremely pleasurable and relaxing to the child and therefore tended to short-circuit the development of a fear response.

These are but a few of the experiments which show that relaxation can not only help extinguish a fear, but also serve as a preventive measure for further development of phobias.

The reverse approach is also true. Especially in children, but also in adults, punishment may serve as a reinforcer for a fear response. Punishing someone or forcing them into the fear-producing situation, without proper therapy, can increase the impact of the phobia.

CHAPTER THREE
What Fear Is and How It Affects The Body

"Our tragedy today is a general and universal physical fear so long sustained by now that we can even bear it . . . the basest of all things is to be afraid."

WILLIAM FAULKNER
Nobel Prize Acceptance Speech,
Stockholm, December, 1950.

In 1939, Mauer, a noted American physician, wrote, "Fear motivates and reinforces behavior that tends to prevent the reoccurance of the fear-producing stimulus." In other words, fear motivates avoidance of a fear-producing stimulus but that very avoidance tends to reinforce the fact that one is afraid. Thus, a self-perpetuating cycle is built up. The woman who has a phobia towards cats, for example, may be constantly avoiding any contact with felines. The conscious avoidance mechanism of cats tends to reinforce her phobic reaction towards them. The more she avoids the object of her fear . . . the greater the impact of the phobia.

The sensation of fear is, first and foremost, a learned self-preservation response, often carefully taught by the mother to the child — such as fear of heat or high places. Such fears of immediate dangers, involving possible body damage or death, are normal human responses.

If you are reacting to a real and present danger, you do not have a "phobia" and there is no reason to get rid of your fear reactions, since the fear is intended to ensure your survival. A phobia, however, refers to strong anxiety caused by a specific object or situation that is not actually dangerous, but which through faulty learning you have conditioned your body to react to with a fearful response.

Real or rational fears include the fear experienced when a person is confronted by a lion or poisonous snake, is caught in a house on fire, involved in an automobile accident, or prior to a risky surgical procedure. These fears develop from real situations which could cause harm to the individual. Most of this type of physical jeopardy is experienced at least once or twice by every person during a lifetime. The fear response in such cases is legitimate and essential for activating the "fight or flight" response which we will discuss in a minute. In no way should people be taught to reduce these types of fear responses. In certain circumstances, fear is a very necessary survival mechanism.

The second type is irrational fear. This fear leads directly to the development of phobic reactions. An example of the development of an irrational fear might be as follows: You are walking along a deserted road and you come across a rattlesnake. You have an immediate fear response and react accordingly to avoid the snake. This is a very logical reaction and the fear is an essential response mechanism. Now, if you notice that any time you walk along a dirt road, you feel anxious and develop the same fear responses as when confronted by the snake, this is considered to be an irrational fear. Developing a phobia towards walking along dirt roads is irrational and unproductive. The illogical fear will serve you effectively to avoid ever walking along dirt roads again and facing a snake under the same circumstances as before. Of course, since no one knows what lies ahead in the future, one cannot predict whether you will be faced by a snake again in some other situation. Very soon, you may find that the phobic reaction has generalized into an avoidance reaction to all roads. You may even find that a fear reaction has generalized to anything related to roads. People have been known to develop a fear of sidewalks, driveways, and even walkways, stemming from an initial fear of dirt roads.

Irrational fears are experienced by every person at some time during their life. Jacqueline Bisset had to overcome her fears during the filming of the movie "The Deep." A major part of her role demanded that she skin dive. The director, Peter Yates, revealed that her fear of water was so great that she was not only afraid of learning how to dive, but was extremely fearful of even getting her head wet. Eventually Jacqueline Bisset gritted her teeth and proceded with the movie. It would have been much simpler if she had been given a program to reduce her fear of water before the filming. This would have made it much easier for her to follow through with her part.

Several years ago, by the Yale Daily News Magazine reported on the fears of celebrities. The magazine asked well-known people around the the world to respond to the question: "What are you most afraid of?" Some of the responses were surprising. John Wayne stated he had a "hell of a lot of respect for wind, water, fire, and the devastation they cause." Muhammad Ali said that he was afraid of dying. English novelist and critic Anthony Burgess stated that he was afraid of what awaited him after death. Barbara Walters responded that violence, kidnapping and being misquoted were prominent fears for her.

Lloyd Bridges has stated that he is extremely fearful of dying and is quoted as saying: "I have no doubt that the fear of death is man's most basic fear — the one he discovers first and the one that is most difficult to overcome." Actor Clint Walker has reported that he is afraid of making the same mistake twice. He goes on to state that after making a mistake he is fearful of not learning from the experience. Anne Francis states that she has always been afraid that her children would be hurt and that if something happened to her, no one would be around to help take care of them. Actress-singer Mitzi Gaynor is afraid of heights. Actor Edward Asner fears that he will not have the courage to speak up or act decisively when such action is needed.

The list goes on and on and I am sure each one of you reading this book could add considerably to the events, things, situations, and aspects of life which produce fear in you.

Some people, who have fears that have gone unresolved for many, many years and spread into numerous other functions of their life, will develop neurotic defense mechanisms, in order to maintain some sense of rational order in their lives. These neurotic defense mechanisms may take the form of irrational avoidance behaviors. The person who is afraid to ride in elevators, not because of the mechanism of an elevator, but because it will force him to be in close proximity to other people he does not know, has developed a phobic reaction to allow him to avoid riding in elevators. It effectively prevents the uncomfortable fear-producing situation of being in a crowded space with people he does not know.

If you are one of the people who goes through life repressing and denying that you have any fear responses, then you may be like the pressure cooker without any safety valve. By keeping things inside and not dealing with them, you tend to build up more and more pressure within. This pressure may take the form of anxiety, ulcers, nervous habits or tics, and it is quite likely that at some time the pressure cooker will explode.

Repression is a form of avoidance and will prevent you coming into contact with the object or situation that you fear. Soon, this repression develops into a phobia and you no longer have an accurate idea as to whether the fear is justified.

Take the example of a young woman who went on an airplane ride for the first time. The plane flew through quite a lot of turbulence and the trip was very unpleasant. She experienced many fear responses during that flight. Not wanting to experience the same fears over again, she avoided all airplane flights in the future. This avoidance, which is a form of repression, prevents her from ever having to fly again. She therefore has developed a phobic reaction towards flying without ever trying a second time. The more she avoids flying, the stronger the fear and phobic response will become.

When you maintain this type of avoidance behavior, you never reach the point of discovering whether your fear is a real or irrational one. You tend to be very restricted and self-limiting in your activities. The avoidance may even cause a distressing conflict to arise if you are required to fly in the future.

Many scientists feel that the act of repression may interfere with certain mental processes which are needed for full functioning of the human psyche. When you repress a significant number of events in your life, the self-limiting nature of your activities may cause you to lose the ability to make decisions rationally. Studies have shown that people who repress fears may develop non-assertive behavior, which simply adds to the vicious circle of fear and phobia repression.

Joan is typical of the non-assertive housewife, who developed a phobia towards losing her husband or incurring his anger. She was a good wife and an excellent mother. She and Ray had been married for ten years and to all their friends, the marriage was close to ideal. Socially, they were well accepted and the children were both doing well in school. Even her closest friends would have been aghast to find out how truly unhappy Joan was.

Her dissatisfaction did not come from an inadequate sex life, nor did she desire to begin a career of her own, outside the house.

The changes had occurred so subtly over the previous ten years that Joan was not really aware of the pattern of behavior which had developed. Coming into the marriage with a definite fear of people and authority, a fear of losing security, and a fear of facing the world alone, led to the development of a non-assertive pattern of behavior. Her husband was not mean or overly demanding, but over the years, she had trained his behavior to conform with her non-assertive behavior. He made all the decisions in the family and even if he were to ask her opinion, she would answer only with a solution that would conform with his usual line of thinking.

The strength of her own personality diminished significantly, even in her own estimation.

Joan was afraid that if she stood up to her husband he might possibly reject her and therefore her worst fears would be realized.

When I first met Joan it was very difficult to get a true picture of the marital situation. Then when her husband arrived for a session and I was able to observe the interaction between the two of them, the problem became quite evident. I immediately began the fear reduction program with Joan and at the same time inserted suggestions for developing a more assertive pattern of behavior. By combining these two therapies, Joan was able to control her fears and at the same time replace the fear evoking behavior with the more assertive patterns of reaction.

It was extremely important to provide Joan with assertiveness training. Once she was able to overcome her fear of losing her husband, assertiveness needed to be immediately inserted into her repertoire of behaviors. Through many years of repressing her fear reactions, a vicious circle of non-assertive behavior had developed. The more fearful she became, the more fear she repressed, and the more non-assertive she became. The chain of behaviors needed to be broken by learning new reactions.

Joan's therapy took several months to complete, but even after the first session, she was able to see positive results from the reorganization of her past behavior patterns to a new assertiveness. During a later session, Ray remarked that his wife had become more challenging and intriguing as a marital partner. Statements such as this seemed to reassure Joan that she was not going to lose her husband by standing up for certain beliefs which she had.

It is interesting to note that many non-assertive behaviors, which have evolved from repressed fear reactions, can eventually lead to the object or action which the individual fears the most.

If Joan had maintained her non-assertive behavior, then her

husband might have become so disinterested in her as a person, that divorce could easily have been the result.

Repressed fear acts like a powerful magnet. It tends to draw closer that which we are trying to avoid.

BODY RESPONSE:

When man is confronted with a real danger or life-threatening situation, his body mobilizes for a "fight or flight" response in order to protect himself. The "fight or flight" response is controlled by the brain and may take only fractions of a second to initiate. First, the adrenal glands are stimulated to pump adrenalin into the bloodstream. This puts the body on the alert to a possibly traumatic situation. Reaction time is speeded up, thinking is faster, the entire body metabolism increases. The brain simultaneously sends signals to take blood from the kidneys and bowels and re-distribute it into the muscles of the arms and legs. The blood vessels in the arms and legs dilate or open up and this increased flow of blood provides more energy to the muscles in the arms and legs.

Other body functions are also changed simultaneously: increase in the rate and strength of the heartbeat; release of stored red blood cells to carry the increased oxygen supply; contraction of the spleen; deepening of respiration and dilation of the bronchi in the lungs to make more oxygen available; redistribution of the blood supply from the skin and the body organs to the muscles and the brain; release of stored sugar from the liver for the use of muscles; and dilation of the pupils.

Within a matter of minutes, all of these responses take place in the acute phobic reaction. If the body is continuously stimulated to respond in this way, the long-term effects may be devastating.

CHRONIC PHOBIC REACTION

Dr. Hans Selye and others have studied the long-term effects of stress. Their findings point to drastic changes within the body brought about by chronic phobias. When faced with a chronic phobic reaction (or CPR) the body is constantly mobilized for quick action — the "fight or flight" response becomes the normal mode of behavior.

It is noteworthy that man is the only animal who seems to suffer from a chronic phobic response. Although other members of the animal kingdom experience acute fear reactions, they do not develop into chronic problems. Man alone, because of his imaginative capabilities, nurtures the chronic phobic reaction.

The chronic phobic reaction develops over a period of time. The main component of this reaction appears to be that the individual suffers from a fear over a period of time and with some frequency. The man who has a chronic phobic reaction towards women will surely be faced with women during a portion of his daily activities. Thus, total avoidance of women would be impossible. Faced with his phobia on a daily basis, the man will display many symptoms of the acute phobic reaction on a regular basis. Gradually, his phobia becomes a chronic problem.

If phobias go unresolved over a period of weeks, months, and even years, then the person is subjecting himself to the possibility of developing a chronic emotional response mechanism. Chronic phobic reactions are characterized by a number of conditions, all of which are due to an increased level of anxiety or fearfulness. Its dominant effects are psychological and physical sensations. These may vary somewhat from one individual to another, but every person with a true phobia will experience a combination of mind-body reactions. The most important of these responses are verbal, muscular and body responses, such as stuttering, excessively fast and shallow breathing leading to dizziness, and functional gastro-intestinal disorders, such as diarrhea. The following represent the major physical and psychological components of the chronic phobic reaction:

Fatigue: You may feel tired from the time of getting up in the morning until going to bed at night. It does not matter how much sleep you get the night before, by the middle of the morning you are extremely fatigued. This "dragged-out" feeling tends to persist during the entire day.

Restlessness: There is a definite feeling of restlessness or a pacing quality to your behavior. You cannot sit down but have to be doing something, anything, in order to keep active.

Tension: Tension is a neuromuscular response. Stated simply, this means that your muscles are contracted and you may notice that you are sitting with your shoulders pulled up towards your ears and the muscles along the back of your neck are very tight and constricted. Your hands may be clenched and after a short period of time, muscular aches and pains, particularly headache and backaches, will develop.

Irritability: Little things which normally would not bother you become very irritating. You notice a shortening of your temper, and have very little tolerance for disturbances, which may include noises, interruptions, and even bright lights. Every day we are bombarded by television, radio, and other news media with the virtues of over-the-counter medications which can eliminate irratibility. The main drawback to most of these is that they only treat the symptom and do nothing to resolve the cause of the discomfort.

Feelings of apprehension: There is a feeling of uneasiness, which may even reach the point of "impending doom." You cannot pick out any one thing in particular which makes you feel uneasy. There is that generalized feeling of fearfulness regarding some upcoming event.

Tension headaches: Tension headaches seem to start in the back of the neck and move up the back of the head. When they become severe, they may even affect eyesight and cause nausea. Try a little test. Reach up and press on the muscles along the back of your neck and the tops of your shoulders. If these feel tight and there is a painful sensation as you apply pressure, then there's a good chance that these muscles are very tight due to tension. You are a prime candidate for the tension headache aspect of fear reduction therapy.

Palpitations of the heart: This causes a feeling of extreme discomfort. It feels as though your heart is missing a beat or is flopping around in your chest. These palpitations are almost always due solely to a chronic phobic reaction.

P. A. T. — These letters stand for paroxysmal atrial tachycardia. This is a very fancy name for an occurrence in which the heart rate very suddenly increases to as much as 200 to 300 beats per minute instead of an average of 70. This response can be extremely frightening to the individual who is suffering from it. The P. A. T. response is triggered by the acute phobic reaction and the continued fear response maintains this frightening reaction.

Shortness of breath: You may notice this shortness of breath with even the most mild physical exertion. Although you may be in good physical condition, even the act of climbing stairs will cause you to gasp for breath. There are basically two reasons for this type of reaction. (1) Because you are involved in a chronic fear situation, you will probably lessen your physical activity level and therefore your physical condition and endurance will deteriorate. Thus, even minor physical activity will cause a shortness of breath. (2) Breathing fast is common in both acute and chronic phobic reactions. This may present a somewhat frightening situation. In order to promote proper functioning of the lungs, there should always be a proper mixture of gases. When a chronic phobic reaction takes place, quicker, more shallow breathing may be triggered. Eventually this quick, shallow breathing eliminates much of the oxygen from the lungs and carbon dioxide builds up. When this improper balance occurs, you will feel short of breath and begin to breathe even quicker. This increased rate of breathing will cause the imbalance to become more severe, in a spiralling reaction, and you will experience dizziness, chest pains, numbness around the lips, hands and perhaps over the whole body, blurry vision and headache. If it is not corrected, you will eventually pass out. Of course when you do pass out, breathing returns to normal and symptoms disappear. Thus the body has a built-in defense mechanism. Unfortunately, however, the chronic phobic reaction may still remain and eventually you will experience the same adverse effects again. This condition is treated very simply, by placing a paper bag over the mouth and nose. You breathe in and out for a period of three to four minutes, re-breathing your own gases and the gas mixture in the lungs becomes re-adjusted.

Trembling: There are certain neurological conditions which may cause trembling, such as cerebral palsy or Parkinson's disease. But, most of the fine trembling which we see in the chronically fearful individual is due entirely to the anxiety reaction elicited by the phobia. Nervous tics may also appear under stress.

Chest pain: This is usually part of the hyperventilation or fast breathing which as been mentioned earlier.

Dizziness: This may be caused by hyperventilation. Also, many people who have chronic phobic reactions develop problems with their neck due to the constant muscular tension in that part of their body. This has been known to trigger a reflex which may cause dizziness and blurry vision.

Sweating: There are several different forms of sweating seen in people with chronic phobic reactions. Sweating of the palms is usually a manifestation of the fear response. The other response is night sweats. I have worked with people who literally soak their bed at night due to sweating. In the absence of fever, there is only one other disease which would cause such extensive night sweats and that is tuberculosis. Since the incidence of tuberculosis has diminished dramatically, most people who have uncontrollable night sweats can attribute it to a chronic phobic reaction.

Gastro-intestinal symptoms: Usually there is a definite loss in appetite with associated feelings of heartburn, nausea and sometimes vomiting. There may be a feeling of butterflies or abdominal fluttering. Constipation and diarrhea are also very prevalent. We notice that these two symptoms tend to alternate, first one, then the other. There may be a week or two weeks of diarrhea, then a week to two weeks of constipation and this alternation may continue back and forth over an extended period of time.

All of the symptoms mentioned above are usually effects of chronic phobic reactions which can be seen or are readily experienced by the person with the phobic reaction. There are many additional bodily reactions, of which you would not be completely aware, which are definite components of the total chronic phobic reaction syndrome. Most of these physiological changes which occur within the body can be measured as a direct result of chronic fear reactions.

In conditions of chronic phobic reactions, we can measure an increase in the body's excretion of nitrogen, phosphorus and potassium, for example.

These three chemicals are essential for the proper functioning of the human body and in particular nitrogen, because it is the essential building block of the body. It is the key portion of protein. Without the proper amount of protein, you are unable to repair damaged tissue. If your body ever gets into a negative nitrogen balance (more nitrogen goes out than comes in), then your body will not be able to repair damaged tissue effectively and can become very susceptible to chronic illnesses.

Phosphorus and potassium are important in muscle metabolism and in maintaining the proper balance of salt and water in the body. Therefore, a loss of these substances in excessive amounts can affect total body functioning.

During the chronic phobic reaction, there is an increased retention of salt in the body. This may lead to swelling or edema in some people, most commonly toward the end of the day around the ankles. Recent studies have shown that edema causes stress. This becomes a cyclical reaction since the chronic phobic reaction causes an increase in the retention of salt, which leads to edema, which leads to an increase in tension.

In the blood, there is a decrease of two types of cells: eosinophils and lymphocytes. Eosinophils are instrumental in your ability to fight allergies. Therefore, you are more susceptible to allergic reactions during times of chronic phobic reactions.

The lymphocytes are directly connected to your ability to fight off viral infections.

There is an increase in the blood sugar. Some borderline diabetics, during CPR, experience elevated blood sugar levels to the point where they become symptomatic diabetics.

There are definite increases in cholesterol. This can probably provide a partial explanation as to why stroke and heart attacks are common among people who are constantly fearful and anxiety-ridden.

There is a decrease in globulin in the blood. This is a form of protein and its reduced level is probably explained by excessive excretion of nitrogen, which is necessary for its production.

There are definite changes in the secretions within the intestinal tract. It is a well-known fact that ulcers are directly connected to chronic anxiety and fear. Hydrochloric acid, which is normally secreted by the stomach, to help digest food, pours out continuously when a person is experiencing a chronic phobic reaction. After the food is gone, the acids work to dissolve the lining of the stomach and ulcers may develop.

The chronic phobic reaction also causes a change in other elements of the blood, mainly cortisone and adrenalin. When you experience a chronic condition of fear, the levels of these substances are elevated, not to the point of an acute phobic reaction, but above the normal level. Why should this be bad for the body? Well, eventually it depletes the adrenal gland. It is extremely important if we are to have a proper "fight or flight" response, that reserves of cortisone and adrenalin be kept in the adrenal glands. If we have depleted this reserve, we will not respond as fast, act as fast, think as fast, in time of emergency, due to this depletion.

There are definite changes in the pituitary and hypothalamus glands. Changes in these glands cause reactions throughout the body. The drastic effects of prolonged chronic phobic reactions may be responsible for a reduction in the secretion by the anterior pituitary or gonadotropic hormones, which in turn stimulate the testes to secrete androgen and the ovary to secrete the hormones, estrogen and progesterone. In the male, there is a reduction in the production of sperm, a decrease in the secretion by the testes of testosterone (the male sex hormone) and a delay or complete suppression of puberty.

In the female, there is a disruption or diminishment of the menstrual cycle, a decrease in uterine weight, and many times a failure to ovulate or failure of the fertilized ovum to become implanted in the uterine wall. This may account for the increased number of spontaneous abortions, infertility and failures in lactation of women who suffer from chronic phobic reactions. Scientists also believe that some post-menopausal reactions are due to chronic anxiety and fear.

During periods of CPR, we see atrophy of the thymus gland, which is located in the chest. This is an autonomic gland and we still are not sure exactly what the function of this gland is. Many scientists feel that this gland has a direct relationship to our immune response to all types of disease conditions. This may even include cancer. It appears that there may be a direct correlation between chronic phobic reaction and a decrease in the effectiveness of this gland.

During this chronic condition, we see a gradual increase in blood pressure, leading to hypertension or high blood pressure. Hypertension is a definite problem in today's society. Most people are not fully aware that if we were to take 100 people with high blood pressure, only five percent would have an identifiable cause for their high blood pressure. The remaining 95 percent would have "essential" hypertension, which means that there is no specific cause for their increased blood pressure. The fear/anxiety reaction may help explain a good number of these cases.

Why such a high incidence of essential hypertension in CPR people? Well, if you remember our discussion on the acute phobic reaction, we mentioned that adrenalin and cortisone pour out into the bloodstream which, in turn, cause a dilation or opening of the blood vessels in the arms, legs and heart. This allows the blood to flow there more easily.

In chronic stress, exactly the opposite occurs. There's a constriction or narrowing down of all the blood vessels peripherally (arms and legs). This means that in order for the blood to get to these places, the heart must pump harder and an increase in blood pressure will result.

In some people, the acute phobic reaction may be so severe as to cause bradycardic syncope or a slowing down of the heart rate, leading to fainting. An example of this would be found in people who are afraid of blood or injections. Thus, fainting becomes a very effective avoidance in the presence of such a phobic stimulus.

In contrast, many people experiencing a chronic phobic reaction will suffer from tachycardia (speeding up of the heart) in the presence of such a phobic stimuli.

You should now be well aware of the fact that acute and chronic phobic reactions affect not just one part of the body, but may affect many functions within the body, all of these being inter-related as a total functioning system. All of these are a high price to pay for something which you can change by practicing the methods which will be outlined in later chapters of this book.

Take a moment to think about your reactions to phobic situations. In a later chapter, you will be able to rate your phobic reactions and determine exactly how they affect your body.

Please bear in mind as you progress through the book that developing a system for the reversal of phobic reactions will take a commitment on your part to follow the program.

A SUMMARY OF BODY RESPONSES TO FEAR
Check the responses you feel periodically or continuously

1. Feeling of panic.
2. Feeling of impending doom.
3. Apprehension.
4. Loss of interest.

5. Difficulty concentrating.
6. Dryness of mouth.
7. Nausea.
8. Vomiting.
9. Tenseness.
10. Vague sinking feeling in abdomen.
11. Diarrhea.
12. Constipation.
13. Urinary frequency.
14. Lightheadedness.
15. Sense of fullness in stomach.
16. Palpitations.
17. Unceasing worry.
18. Amenorrhea (failure to menstruate regularly).
19. Sleep disturbance.
20. Lack of pleasure.
21. Indigestion or upset stomach.
22. Irritability (shortness of temper).
23. Sense of pressure on the chest.
24. Impotence.
25. Nightmares.
26. Incapacity to relax.
27. Sense of choking or suffocating.
28. Decreased appetite.
29. Episodic panic attacks.
30. Restlessness.
31. Impatience.
32. Hyperactivity.
33. Hyperventilation.
34. Sweaty palms.
35. Tremor.
36. Tachycardia (fast heart beat).
37. Increased muscle tension.
38. Fidgety movements of the hands.
39. Irregular breathing.
40. Facial tics or grimacing.

CHAPTER FOUR
Are You One of These?
Phobia Identification

> "Fear of ideas makes us impotent
> and ineffective."
> WILLIAM O. DOUGLAS,
> "The Manifest Destiny of America"
> The Progressive, February, 1955

It should be obvious to you by now that you are not alone in your fears. Over 10 million Americans have obsessive fears about something, and the list includes more than 200 examples — which you can find at the end of the book.

In a survey of three thousand U.S. inhabitants, these were the most prominent fears reported:

1. Speaking before a group — 41%
2. Heights — 32%
3. Insects and bugs — 22%
4. Financial problems — 22%
5. Deep water — 22%
6. Sickness — 19%
7. Death — 19%
8. Flying — 18%

9. Loneliness — 14%
10. Dogs — 11%
11. Driving/riding in a car — 9%
12. Darkness — 8%
13. Elevators — 8%
14. Escalators — 5%

According to the London *Sunday Times,* which reported this American survey, "women are generally more fearful than men." Twice as many women as men were fearful of heights, insects, deep water, flying or driving in cars; three times as many women were frightened of darkness; four times as many were frightened of elevators. They were more fearful of dogs, of getting sick, and of dying. But if that makes it seem like a male chauvinist survey, it is worth noting that men fear financial problems more often than women do.

Many people repress their fears to such an extent, however, that they are no longer consciously aware of having them. Their body signals fear to them, but their mind refuses to acknowledge its presence.

The first step, then, in resolving phobias requires intelligent detective work to pinpoint the type and degree of phobia from which you suffer. You are due a pat on the back at this point. By coming this far in the book, you have shown a true commitment to beginning the process of resolving your fears. No longer will fear be a controlling force in your life.

You may ask yourself if we are going to rid you of all fear reactions. The answer is a definitive — NO! Each one of us needs to operate at a certain level of tolerable, nonpathological fear reactions. These fear reactions keep us safe from danger and sometimes may even spur us on to higher levels of achievement. We need a healthy equilibrium between normal psychological and physical functioning and necessary fear reactions.

As I have said, some fears are needed and are of a beneficial nature. As psychologist Leonard Zunin says in his book:

I believe that courage is all too often mistakenly seen as the absence of fear. If you descend by a rope from a cliff and are not fearful to some degree, you are either crazy or unaware. Courage is seeing your fear in a realistic perspective, defining it, considering the alternatives and choosing to function in spite of the risk.*

The purpose of this book is to help you develop the skills and courage to deal with your fears as you experience them. You will be learning to see your fears in a proper perspective so that they are not blown out of proportion to the actual risks which are involved. In addition, you will also be given a method for reducing the phobic reactions which have developed from an unrealistic perspective of your fear responses. It is my hope that after you have finished this book, you will be able to deal effectively with the fears presented during normal life situations and get rid of any phobic reactions which inhibit your ability to enjoy life and reach your full potential.

In the next several chapters, you will become acquainted with certain methods of relaxation, which we will use to counter the fear reactions.

I would be sitting in a luxurious summer cottage located on Paradise Island, in the Bahamas, if I had a dollar for each patient who informed me that he or she is able to relax all of the time, but still has problems developing from fear reactions.

Their statements usually run something like the following: "Listen doctor, I can relax anytime I want. I sleep well at night and relaxation is really easy for me."

These are the people who assume that resting in front of the television set or painting an oil picture, or lying next to a swimming pool, are the types of relaxation needed to overcome the fear response. It is true that certain portions of these relaxing situations are important for some reduction of stress and fear, but they only scratch the surface. Relaxation which is not programmed becomes a very hit and miss therapeutic method. The

*Leonard Zunin and Natalie Zunin, *Contact: The First Four Minutes* (New York-Nash Publishing Corporation, 1972), p. 23.

deep relaxation which we are going to teach you in the next chapters will bring about physical changes in your body, which are the exact opposite of those changes brought about by fear.

Usually it takes only a few sessions of practicing the relaxation methods for my patients to realize that what they thought was relaxation was, in reality, only a minor reduction in muscular tension. By the end of this book, you will be able to relax both mentally and physically at will and to the greatest degree possible.

It is now time to start the process of unravelling your fears by completing instrument number one — the Fear Inventory. In order to re-use it several times, I suggest that you photocopy the page or transfer your answers onto a plain sheet of paper. The tests may indicate that you have only one phobia (such as fear of elevators), or a multiple phobia. If more than one phobia is indicated, then your task may take slightly longer and be somewhat more involved. Don't get discouraged. A positive attitude is your best ammunition to fight off defeat. Always work one step at a time.

Even if you know what your fears are, complete the fear inventory anyway. You may be surprised to find out that you have overlapping fears or that one major fear has concealed other, less important ones.

The following represents a list of some of the more common phobias. Put a check mark beside any of the things or situations that cause you to experience a feeling of fear or other unpleasant sensations — such as knotting of the stomach or breathlessness. Try to imagine each of the statements mentally as you work through the list.

Fear Inventory

— 1. High places
— 2. Being shut up in a confined space
— 3. Animals
— 4. Airplanes
— 5. The night
— 6. Lightning
— 7. Fish
— 8. Blood
— 9. Sounds
—10. Open spaces

___11. Spiders
___12. Sex
___13. Birds
___14. Success
___15. Failure
___16. Women
___17. Men
___18. Insects
___19. Sleep
___20. Stairs
___21. Needles
___22. Test
___23. Snakes
___24. Thunder
___25. Water
___26. Work
___27. Being alone
___28. Sunlight
___29. Glass
___30. Dawn
___31. Fire
___32. High objects
___33. Trains
___34. Snow
___35. Disease

___36. Meeting people
___37. Darkness
___38. Knives
___40. Doctors
___41. Giving a speech
___42. Dogs
___43. Cats
___44. Being touched
___45. Marriage
___46. Performing in front of
    a group
___48. Falling
___49. Automobiles
___49. People in authority
___50. Being watched while
    working
___51. Weapons
___52. Dirt
___53. Fire
___54. Feeling rejected
___55. Kissing
___56. Financial problems
___57. Criticism
___58. Change
___59. Pain

If you have checked any of the statements, then you may have a phobic reaction to that object or situation. To verify the presence of that fear, proceed with the more detailed fear inventory below for 20 of the most common phobias. You may find you have more than one. If a fear you have is not listed, jot down aspects of that fear that cause you to experience unpleasant feelings.

Fear Inventory
Work each group separately. Each of the statements below refers to things that may cause you to experience fear or related unpleasant sensations. Read each statement carefully and answer either yes or no.

1. Performophobia — fear of speaking before a group
   I AM FEARFUL OF . . .
   a. Speaking in front of a group   Yes___ No___
   b. Having people watch me   Yes___ No___
   c. Making mistakes in front of a group   Yes___ No___
   d. Standing up before a group   Yes___ No___

2. Acrophobia — fear of high places
   I AM FEARFUL OF . . .
   a. Ladders   Yes___ No___
   b. Tall buildings   Yes___ No___
   c. Bridges   Yes___ No___
   d. Looking out a window in a   Yes___ No___
      tall building

3. Acarophobia — fear of insects
   I AM FEARFUL OF . . .
   a. Flies   Yes___ No___
   b. Seeing bugs   Yes___ No___
   c. Touching bugs   Yes___ No___
   d. Roaches   Yes___ No___

4. Fear of Financial Problems
   I AM FEARFUL OF . . .
   a. Losing my job   Yes___ No___
   b. Overdrawing my checking account   Yes___ No___
   c. Not having enough money to   Yes___ No___
      pay bills
   d. Not having any savings   Yes___ No___

5. Hydrophobia — fear of water
   I AM FEARFUL OF . . .
   a. Swimming   Yes___ No___
   b. Putting my head under water   Yes___ No___
   c. Swimming under water   Yes___ No___
   d. Taking a bath or shower   Yes___ No___

6. Fear of Sickness
   I AM FEARFUL OF . . .
   a. People with colds   Yes___ No___
   b. Having a temperature   Yes___ No___
   c. Talking about sickness   Yes___ No___
   d. Seeing sick people   Yes___ No___

7. Fear of Death
I AM FEARFUL OF . . .
- a. Funerals   Yes___ No___
- b. Talking about death   Yes___ No___
- c. Seeing dead people   Yes___ No___
- d. Thinking about people who   Yes___ No___
  have died

8. Airplane Phobia—fear of flying
I AM FEARFUL OF . . .
- a. Airplane flights   Yes___ No___
- b. Seeing airplanes take off   Yes___ No___
- c. Watching airplanes land   Yes___ No___
- d. Flying at night   Yes___ No___

9. Fear of Loneliness
I AM FEARFUL OF . . .
- a. Being alone   Yes___ No___
- b. Not being invited out   Yes___ No___
- c. Not having someone to love   Yes___ No___
- d. Not having friends   Yes___ No___

10. Zoophobia—fear of animals
I AM FEARFUL OF . . .
- a. Touching animals   Yes___ No___
- b. Hearing animals   Yes___ No___
- c. Being touched by animals   Yes___ No___
- d. Seeing animals   Yes___ No___

11. Fear of Riding in a Car
I AM FEARFUL OF . . .
- a. Driving a car   Yes___ No___
- b. Sitting in the front seat of a car   Yes___ No___
- c. Riding in a car at night   Yes___ No___
- d. Riding in a car in heavy traffic   Yes___ No___

12. Noctophobia—fear of night
I AM FEARFUL OF . . .
- a. The coming of dusk   Yes___ No___
- b. Seeing the moon   Yes___ No___
- c. Going to sleep   Yes___ No___
- d. The hours of darkness   Yes___ No___

13. Climacophobia—fear of stairs/elevators/escalators
I AM FEARFUL OF . . .

    a. Escalators   Yes__ No__
    b. Steep stairs   Yes__ No__
    c. Winding stairs   Yes__ No__
    d. Steps without a handrail   Yes__ No__

14. Claustrophobia—fear of being shut up in a confined space
I AM FEARFUL OF . . .

    a. Rooms with no windows   Yes__ No__
    b. Elevators   Yes__ No__
    c. Small rooms   Yes__ No__
    d. Tunnels   Yes__ No__

15. Kakorrhaphiophobia—fear of failure
I AM FEARFUL OF . . .

    a. Getting fired   Yes__ No__
    b. Not getting a raise   Yes__ No__
    c. Not achieving my goals   Yes__ No__
    d. Not getting a promotion   Yes__ No__

16. Hemotophobia—fear of blood
I AM FEARFUL OF . . .

    a. Seeing someone else's blood   Yes__ No__
    b. Seeing my own blood   Yes__ No__
    c. Seeing an operation   Yes__ No__
    d. Reading about blood   Yes__ No__

17. Arachneophobia—fear of spiders
I AM FEARFUL OF . . .

    a. Touching spiders   Yes__ No__
    b. Seeing spiders   Yes__ No__
    c. Reading about spiders   Yes__ No__
    d. Being bitten by a spider   Yes__ No__

18. Testaphobia—fear of tests
I AM FEARFUL OF . . .

    a. Small quizzes   Yes__ No__
    b. Final examinations   Yes__ No__
    c. Studying for a test   Yes__ No__
    d. Failing a test   Yes__ No__

19. **Ophidiophobia**—fear of snakes
    I AM FEARFUL OF . . .
    a. Seeing pictures of snakes   Yes__ No__
    b. Seeing a live snake   Yes__ No__
    c. Touching a harmless snake   Yes__ No__
    d. Touching a snake's cage   Yes__ No__

20. **Belonephobia**—fear of needles
    I AM FEARFUL OF . . .
    a. Being injected   Yes__ No__
    b. Pins   Yes__ No__
    c. Knitting needles   Yes__ No__
    d. Watching people being injected   Yes__ No__

MEASURING THE INTENSITY OF YOUR FEAR

Now turn to the *Fear Intensity Profile*. Using a separate sheet of paper, rate the intensity of your fear or fears.

Take your time — don't rush through the forms. Think carefully about each of the answers.

FEAR INTENSITY PROFILE

Place a check mark next to each of the reactions that you experience when thinking or experiencing the phobic situation. The intensity of more than one phobia may be determined with this form. Each phobia should be worked separately.

Reaction	Phobia 1	Phobia 2	Phobia 3	Phobia 4
1. HANDS COLD				
2. HANDS SWEATY				
3. TIGHT STOMACH				
4. ACID STOMACH				
5. PALPITATIONS				

6. QUAVERING VOICE

7. FACE FLUSHES

8. BACKACHE

9. FACE FEELS HOT

10. CONSTIPATION

11. HANDS SHAKE

12. SPEEDING UP HEART

13. LEGS SHAKE

14. SHALLOW, RAPID BREATHING

15. SHORTNESS OF BREATH

16. BLURRY VISION

17. NEED TO URINATE

18. GASSINESS

19. BURPING

20. DIARRHEA

21. LIGHT HEADED

22. FEET COLD

23. FEET SWEATY

24. HEADACHE

TOTAL CHECKS

Now, add all the check marks for each column. This will be your Fear Intensity Profile for each phobia. This score will tell you if the phobia reaction is: mild, 1 to 8, moderate, 8 to 16, or severe, 16 to 24.

As you proceed through the following chapters and immerse yourself in the Fear Reduction Program, you will readily become aware of the power your mind has not only over your thinking, but also over how you feel physically. Chapter 3 spent a considerable amount of time pointing out the negative effects of anxiety and stress on the body, which are brought about by uncontrolled fear. Scientists and physicians are now reassessing the effect that thoughts and emotions have on such diseases as multiple sclerosis, cancer and diseases of the heart and blood vessels. But these thoughts and ideas regarding the effect the mind has on the disease process are not in any way new. Daniel Hack Tuke, a London physician, spoke at length regarding these connections in his book, *Illustrations of the Influence of the Mind Upon the Body, 1884*. In this work he concluded:

> "We have seen that the influence of the mind on the body is not transient power; that in health it may exalt sensory functions, or suspend them altogether; excite the nervous system so as to cause the various forms of convulsive action of the voluntary muscles, or repress it so as to render them powerless; may stimulate or paralyze the muscles of organic life, and the processes of Nutrition and Secretion — causing even death; in disease it may restore the functions which it takes away in health, reinnervating the sensory and motor nerves, exciting healthy vascularity and nervous power, and assisting the vis midicatrix Naturae to throw off disease action or absorb morbid deposits."

Although Tuke's language may be somewhat old-fashioned, his basic thought is becoming a cornerstone in the treatment of psychological and stress disorders. We are well aware of the fact that the thought process can control health even to the extent of causing death. The "will to live" is no myth, but a scientific fact. These principles have been used for centuries among various cultures, with voodoo being a prime example.

Thus, if you become extremely scared of flying, for example, and someone tells you "it's all in your head," they're essentially correct. The thought process and initial reaction originates within your own mental processes and may negatively influence your physical functioning.

Combine mental fear with its physical effects and you have an individual who is going to suffer greatly and enjoy life less and less.

Keep in mind the correlation between what you think and how you feel, as you proceed with the fear intensity profile.

Become Aware

- of what you tell yourself
- of your own behaviors
- of unrealistic fears
- of the choices you make

If you have one or more phobias, rate each one individually and your composite score for each fear will give you the order of importance of the phobia reduction process.

The phobic reaction which attains the lowest score should be the first phobia with which you deal. Some of you may wonder why I am not telling you to pick the most intense phobia to begin with. The answer is very simple. You need a success experience to increase your motivation for working with the more complicated and stubborn phobias, which scored higher on the list. By starting with a weaker phobic reaction, you give yourself a better chance of successfully completing the therapy process. This process, like anything else, has to be learned through practice and perseverance.

A few years ago I took up skiing with my family and found it to be a very enjoyable and exhilarating experience. My partner started skiing at the same time, but did not take any lessons. While I was on the "bunny hill," he immediately proceeded to an upper level hill and took a crash course from a friend. While he spent time in the lodge having friends sign his cast, my family and I proceeded with the popular graduated length method in which the instructor starts you out on very small skis. It is therefore much easier to learn the fundamentals of skiing and enjoy being successful. Each day the instructor increased the length of our skis to correspond with the skills we were developing. By the end of four days we were on normal length skis and the skills we had acquired were now firmly engrained: more importantly, the total experience was gradual and planned which allowed us continuous measures of success and enjoyment. The following year I convinced my partner to try the graduated length method and I am happy to report that he is now a much better skier and avoided breaking any bones last season.

Each year since the initial set of lessons, I have found that refresher courses are needed to improve my skills. For the same reason we have included aspects of the fear reduction program which need to be practiced regularly.

The program is designed to ensure that you meet with success and develop permanent habits to overcome fear.

Remember, there has never been a concert pianist who fails to practice every single day. The same applies to this program. Along the same lines, a person must learn the music before playing the concert and therefore you must start here, at the beginning. As you work through the phobic reactions, your confidence will build and in a short period of time, the fear reduction program will be forever incorporated in your psychological bag of tricks.

But there are no magic short-cuts, only practice and the genuine desire to change. Learning to walk before you run applies to this program.

Important Note: The only exception to starting with the least anxiety-provoking phobia would be if one of the phobias will be encountered soon, or one of the more intense phobias presently has a very harmful effect on your life. These exceptions should be well thought out before embarking on a course of therapy which starts in the middle or at the top of the fear intensity list. There are always exceptions and some of you may need to start on the second-most, fourth-most, or the most anxiety-provoking phobia immediately. If you have chosen this method, I must repeat again that it is imperative that you have a complete understanding of each step in the fear reduction program before applying this method to the phobia you have chosen.

NEW BEHAVIOR

What you are learning is a new behavior and therefore you must practice diligently. Please do not be so naive as to believe that you will have absolute and complete success on your first attempt to reverse the fear response. You must always keep in mind that:

FAILURE IS ONLY A TRANSITORY SITUATION — ONLY YOU CAN LET IT BECOME A PERMANENT PATTERN OF BEHAVIOR.

Practice may not always make perfect, but it will definitely reduce your fears and make you a much happier and more productive person.

The fear inventory instruments completed, it is time for you to move into the therapy process of fear reduction. The first step will be explained in the next chapter, when you will be introduced to autogenic training, which will be the mainstay of your relaxation and anti-fear process. Since learning to relax to the fullest extent of your capabilities is paramount to reducing fear, you should pay close attention to the next chapter.

The second step of the fear reduction process in Chapter 6 deals with the actual desensitization process. This is the process whereby you will be combining the relaxation training with the fear producing situations or thoughts. The hierarchy which you will construct will be a list of fear-producing events in order of the anxiety they produce, culminating in the phobic experience itself. The information about your fears which you have detailed in this chapter will be used later on in constructing your fear hierarchies.

Please keep in mind that the fear reduction program has been designed to elicit certain behaviors and responses from you. Some of these responses will serve as the building blocks to successful completion of the program and further use of the fear reduction principles in other life situations.

The aim of the program involves:

1. Building positive associations concerning fear reduction.
2. Rewarding yourself for developing fear reducing behaviors.
3. Developing appropriate controls to prevent the reoccurrence of specific fears.
4. Establishing alternative behaviors which are incompatible with your fear response.
5. Increasing your assertive behavior in the face of fear producing situations.

The fear reduction program is extremely intensive in its aim to reduce your fear reactions. As you proceed through the program, certain secondary outcomes will become evident. Some of these secondary outcomes will be:

- a more realistic view of yourself
- increased potential for self change
- increased coping behaviors
- increased work productivity
- increased self confidence
- better and more enjoyable interpersonal relationships
- increased assertive behavior

Of course, you will not be experiencing all of these secondary outcomes from your initial attempts at the fear reduction program. When the program is mastered and you begin to use its basic principles in other aspects of your life, then you will begin to notice a carry-over effect. The method you will learn to counteract the non-productive and distasteful aspects of fear can be used effectively to enhance your present lifestyle and serve as a defense mechanism against the number one emotional and physical crippler — *stress.*

The time has come for you to apply the information you have gained from this chapter and the ones before it. Let's take a moment to review what you should know at this point. You should know:

- How phobias develop
- The effect fear has on your mental and emotional well being
- The effect fears have on your physical health
- What your phobias are
- How intense your phobias are

If you have not yet gained this knowledge, then take some time and go back and review the relevent parts of the book.

At this point in the program, some people may ask, "What if I don't want to put in all the time and energy needed to get rid of my fear? What's going to happen?"

The answer to that question lies in the fundamental formation of fear. Let's take a moment to review how a fear may affect you emotionally, psychologically and physically.

In the most basic context, you are confronted with a fearful situation which is extremely difficult for you to find an answer to — giving a speech or making a presentation at work would be a good example of such a fear. Soon the fear begins to mount as the situation comes closer and closer. Unfortunately, there is a good chance that you will make an unconscious decision to cope with the fear through inappropriate psychological and physical behavior. This behavior may take the form of a migraine headache, which affects you so severely that you are unable to approach the fearful situation. The physical and emotional symptoms are wide and varied, but all serve the purpose of preventing contact with the feared situation.

Anthropologist Gregory Bateson has described this situation as a "double-bind." Many people delaying treatment of a fear problem end up in the "double-bind" situation. In this predicament, you must choose between two unacceptable alternatives, while all the time denying to yourself the true nature of your problem. Your physical and emotional symptoms free you from having to face the feared situation, which you do not know how to manage. Unfortunately, continued unconscious use of these maladaptive symptoms may cause your family and friends to modify their expectations and behaviors towards you. Soon, their total behavior pattern towards you will be changed by your unconscious "double-bind" reaction. Once you develop this pattern of behavior and it proves successful in avoiding what you fear, there is a tendency to imitate the same pattern over and over again when faced with future feared situations. Unfortunately, many of these decisions you make are on an unconscious level and you are not fully aware of the dangerous pattern of behavior you are falling into.

And there you have it, the setting up of a destructive pattern of behavior by not resolving your fears. Of course, there are other reasons for participating in the Fear Reduction Program, but I think that the above information should give you a strong enough reason for proceeding with the next chapter with increased excitement and commitment towards resolving your fears.

CHAPTER FIVE
Autogenics

"The first duty of man is that of subduing fear."

THOMAS CARLYLE
from *Hero and Hero Worship*

By this time, you should have a good idea of the major components of the phobic reaction. Now it is time to talk about the specifics of the technique that you will use to stop your phobic reactions effectively.

HISTORY OF AUTOGENIC METHODS
Autogenic training, which is self-induced relaxation through the repetition of certain exercises and verbal suggestions, was first recognized as a therapeutic method in the early 1900's. A German neuropathologist, Oskar Vogt, and co-worker, Korniniar Brodmann, at the Berlin Neuro-Biological Institute, observed that patients experienced feelings of heaviness and warmth during training in self-hypnosis.

When self-hypnosis was practiced several times a day it tended to reduce anxiety, stress, fatigue and tension. The more patients experienced relief from these symptoms, the quicker they got well.

About the time that Freud had begun to give up using hypnosis, because of its unpredictability, Dr. Johannes Schultz in Germany was developing exercises which would induce heaviness and warmth in the limbs through mental imagery. Schultz felt that too much control was in the hands of the therapist during hypnosis, and proposed that if the patient was able to direct the process himself, then a technique could be developed which would be *self-generating, self-regulating, and self-reinforcing.* Remember these three phrases, for they will be the main force which will allow you to use the Fear Reduction Program.

Schultz found that the autogenic or self-directed technique not only produced effects similar to the hypnotic state, but allowed patients a greater degree of control over their symptoms.

Continued research by Luthe and Schultz led to the development of the six standard exercises which are the cornerstones of the autogenic process. The repetition of key phrases brings about changes in the nerves and muscular system (interpreted as "heaviness" in the arms and legs), the blood vessels (warmth), slower heart rhythm and respiration, increased warmth of the chest and cooling of the forehead. Schultz found the best results were achieved by subjects if they maintained a casual and passive attitude during performance of the exercises. This process has been researched extensively in the United States and in Europe. Luthe and Schultz's books on autogenic training* have been hailed as forerunners to the idea of self-regulation and control of what we normally think of as "automatic" body processes, beyond our voluntary control.

Although research into the use of autogenic training is relatively new, behavioral scientists have been using it extensively for the use of phobia and fear reduction. The autogenic exercises which you will be using later in the book are based at least in part upon the phrases developed by Luthe and Schultz. I have found that these exercises produce certain psychological and physical changes which are required to induce relaxation.

*Wolfgang Luthe and Joannes H. Schultz, *Autogenic Therapy,* Vols. I – VI (New York: Grune and Stratton, Inc.) 1969 – 1970.

On becoming proficient at autogenic training, you will find that the autogenic state is associated with muscular relaxation. Some patients report a reduction in muscular tension immediately upon assuming the training posture.

Doctor Johann Stoyva of the University of Colorado has conducted considerable research into the field of autogenics and points out that:

"In autogenic training, a technique which has been extensively used in treating stress-related disorders, emphasis is placed upon attaining the 'autogenic shift' or Umschaltung — a condition for which passive concentration is held to be absolutely essential. In its physiological aspects, this condition involves a shift to parasympathetic control of the autonomic nervous system — as evidenced by muscle relaxation, slowed heart rate and respiration, and increased skin temperature."

DEFINITION; SYMPATHETIC NERVOUS SYSTEM,
PARASYMPATHETIC AUTONOMIC NERVOUS SYSTEM

The sympathetic nervous system may be called the involuntary nervous system that deals with bodily functions which are not normally under our conscious control, such as maintaining blood pressure, heartbeat, breathing, secretion of bodily fluids and the digestion of food. The parasympathetic or voluntary nervous system is connected directly with the operation of the body muscles connected to bones. For example, if you decide to raise your arm, move your leg, tap your finger or close your mouth, these movements are voluntary and are controlled by the voluntary or parasympathetic nervous system.

When the "fight or flight" response is evoked during phobic reactions the sympathetic nervous system, which is a part of the autonomic or involuntary nervous system, comes into play. The sympathetic nervous system immediately begins secreting certain hormones, such as epinephrine and adrenalin. Other hormones such as noradrenalin or norepinephrine are also secreted into the bloodstream. All of these hormones are directly related to increases in the body's blood pressure, heart rate and increases in the rate of metabolism.

Recently the work of Dr. Elmer Green of the Menninger Foundation in Topeka, Kansas, has focused on better defining the mind-body, self-regulatory functions of autogenic training. Through research with Swami Rama and Jack Schwarz, Green feels that "any physiological process that can be detected and displayed in any objective fashion to the subject can be self-regulated in some degree." He further notes that:

"Putting together some of the pieces of the mind-body system as observed both physiologically in the nervous system and behaviorally (through autogenic feedback training) we have found it convenient to postulate a psychophysiological principal which goes as follows: Every change in the physiological state is accompanied by an appropriate change in the mental-emotional state, conscious or unconscious. Conversely, every change in the mental-emotional state, conscious or unconscious, is accompanied by an appropriate change in the physiological state." (1973)

Stated simply, this means that there is a direct connection between your emotions and the physical functioning of your body. If you are anxious and fearful, then your body will react in an anxious and fearful manner. The reverse is also true; if your body reacts in an anxious and fearful manner, then so too will your emotions be shaped towards anxiety and fear.

AUTOGENIC TRAINING AND ANXIETY REDUCTION
Autogenic training has been found to be an effective way to reduce mental and physical anxiety. Using autogenics combined with systematic desensitization (which will be explained in the next chapter) the vicious circle of fear can be broken. This fear circle is diagrammed below.

Patients report that after the first two to four weeks of autogenic and systematic desensitization training they feel much calmer, get more sleep and feel more refreshed in the morning with lessened aches, pains, general muscle twitching and a sense of relief from fear. My follow-up studies show that there's a continued reduction of the fear and phobic cycle, with related symptoms, over a six to ten-week period.

Follow-up studies conducted several months after initial training show that if the person continues to practice, then the phobic reaction will remain extinguished.

Many of the studies which I refer to have been validated through the use of electromyographic biofeedback. For those of you who are not familiar with biofeedback, this is simply an electronic apparatus which measures the electrical activity of the specific muscle over which the electrode is placed. Every time your

The Vicious Cycle of Fear

Fearful Situation

CHRONIC PHOBIC REACTION

REACTION BASED ON:
A. Personality Factors
B. Past Experiences
C. Experiences by other

INCREASING FEARS

RESPONSE
A. Emotional
B. Physical

CONSTANT THOUGHTS OF THE FEAR

Autogenics to BREAK FEAR CYCLE

AVOIDANCE BEHAVIOR

muscle contracts, electrical impulses are sent out. The machine's sensitive electrodes are placed on the skin to detect and measure these electrical impulses. The more electrical impulses there are, the more tense and contracted the muscle is. The less electrical signals, the more relaxed and fear-free the body is.

An EMG (electromyographic) machine was attached to many of my patients while they were experiencing a phobic reaction. There was a definite increase in muscular tension during the phobic reaction. In contrast, when they learned to elicit a relaxation response, muscle tension was reduced. Before describing the actual exercises themselves, it is essential that you understand what body changes each exercise is designed to elicit. It is my feeling that the more you understand about the reduction of fear, the more successful you will be in overcoming it.

HOW AUTOGENIC EXERCISES AFFECT THE BODY

The use of autogenic training affects both psychological and physical functioning at the same time. This simultaneous training is based on three principles: (1) A reduction in nerve and muscle stimulation; (2) Conditioned mental repetition of specially adapted verbal formulae; and (3) Passive concentration.

First, exercises of the standard formula attempt to induce relaxation in nerves and muscles. This is accomplished through mental imagery of the specific parts of the body and repetition of phrases such as "My right arm is heavy."

What is happening when a muscle becomes heavy? Do your muscles *become* heavy when they *feel* heavy?

Researchers using special devices have recorded definite increases in the weight of arms and legs during the passive concentration exercises on heaviness. This increase in weight can be explained by relaxation of certain muscle groups and an increase in blood flow to that particular area.

Some of the bodily changes which may occur during autogenic training will not be noticed by the patient. Some of these may be so small as to go completely unnoticed. The exercises for warmth to the limbs are intended to increase circulation to the surface of the body. Some researchers have found that the standard exercises for heaviness and warmth have increased warmth in the area of the liver which in turn has raised the subject's blood sugar level. Vaso-dilation of the surface blood vessels is synonymous with a relaxed state.

The cardiac exercise, "My heartbeat is calm and regular," is aimed at increasing the output of the heart and therefore improving blood flow and oxygen exchange throughout the body.

The autogenic formula for respiratory activity, "My breathing is calm and regular," has been shown to produce a better exchange of gasses within the body and to decrease the frequency of breathing. This change in the respiratory function has been most dramatically exhibited in experiments with asthmatic patients who have shown an almost instantaneous normalization of their disturbed pattern of breathing after starting the autogenic training exercises.

We will be using autogenic training specifically to reduce the effects of fear reactions. Although we will not be using autogenics for any therapies, other than phobic reactions, you should be aware that this technique has been effectively used to remedy many other disorders, including disorders of the respiratory tract, gastro-intestinal tract, the circulatory system, endocrine disorders and numerous forms of physical and emotional dysfunction.

THE BASIC TRAINING POSITION

Before starting your autogenic training program, you must learn the basic training position. This position will allow you to obtain the best results and is the most conducive for eliciting autonomic body control.

1. *Environment:* These exercises should be practiced in a fairly quiet environment. This does not mean you must be in a soundproofed room but your place of training should be as free from disturbing noises and interruptions as possible. The room lighting should also be reduced as much as possible. Although your eyes

will be closed, strong light will still penetrate the eyelids and distract your mind away from the exercises.

The chair you sit in should be comfortable and it is advantageous if it can be reclined slightly.

All of the above conditions are considered ideal and you may not be able to duplicate them during each of the practice sessions. At home, it may be easier to control the environment, but when practicing at the office or outside the house you may have to modify some of these requirements.

2. *Training Posture:* After you have become proficient in autogenics to reverse the effects of acute or chronic phobic reactions, you will not have to assume a training position; you will be able to use autogenics while standing, talking, walking and even driving. But for now it is easier to practice the autogenics and desensitization process while sitting in a chair.

Place the book in front of you or in your lap as you read the directions. Follow each of the instructions carefully.

1. Sit forward in the chair to allow as much of the upper part of the leg freedom from support of the chair.
2. Make sure that your knees are bent beyond a 45 degree angle.
3. Allow your arms to hang limply at your sides.
4. Your head should be tilted forward, "like a rag doll," eyes closed. (Of course, you cannot have your eyes closed at this moment.)
5. Wrists should be resting on your thighs, with your hands inward.
6. Adjust your position if any of the above directions are uncomfortable.

While you are in this position, take ten deep breaths, exhaling slowly and fully. Check each of the *parts of your body,* starting with your hands and working down to your feet, to see which muscles are tense and which are relaxed.

1. Hands
2. Biceps (upper arms)
3. The backs of the upper arms (triceps)

4. The forehead and scalp
5. Central face (eyes and nose)
6. Lower face (mouth and jaw)
7. Neck (sides and back)
8. Shoulders (top and back)
9. Stomach (entire abdominal area)
10. Thighs
11. Calves
12. Feet

There are, of course, many other muscles within the body, but these major muscle groups will be the key to relaxing the rest of the body. We will be dealing with them in the order in which I have presented them and, when done properly, there will be a carry-over effect to any other muscles which have not been mentioned.

PROGRESSIVE RELAXATION
This technique of progressive relaxation will be used for the initial training exercise. When Dr. Jacobson first developed this technique in 1938, he devoted up to 200 sessions per patient, teaching the effectiveness of his progressive relaxation.

This technique has been modified hundreds of times by numerous clinicians. The basic principles of his technique are still valid and will serve as a starting point in the relaxation portion of the Fear Reduction Program. He determined that in order to relax a muscle group one must first know how it feels in a tense position. The effect of releasing tension then gives the patient the experience of relaxation.

HOW TO BREATHE WHILE PROCEEDING WITH THE TENSION EXERCISES
It is very important that you know the proper breathing technique while proceeding through the tensing exercises.

- take a deep breath as you tense a particular muscle group.
- as you "hold it," study the tension in that particular muscle group and hold your breath while you are tensing.

- give yourself the silent message "let go" and this will be your signal to relax.
- as you let go of the muscle tension, let your breath out.
- as the breath is let out, resume deep rhythmic breathing and study the difference between the tension and the relaxation.

The words "let go" will gradually become a signal for you to reduce tension. As an example, if you are in a discussion with a friend and you notice that your muscles become tense after he has said something that annoys you, just mentally say to yourself "let go" and as you do, exhale your breath. This will take practice and may not work the first time. But after practicing the exercises and using the "let go" technique in real life situations, you will find that repetition of these words and exhaling your breath will cause the muscles in your body immediately to assume a more relaxed position.

TRAINING SESSION NUMBER 1
Begin this exercise by inhaling a deep breath and as you do, silently repeat the number "one" to yourself. Hold the breath for three seconds and then let it out very slowly, silently repeating the number "one" to yourself again. Repeat this procedure five times. Each time you breath out, notice that there is a slight sag in your body. Your body will feel as though it is sinking down slightly. Let this happen; do not try to force anything. The breathing technique should be the preliminary exercise before any one of the treatment sessions. The breathing exercises can also be used as a quick treatment procedure at any time during the day.

STEP 1
Lie down in the most comfortable position that you can find. If a bed or mat is not available, then try to find a comfortable chair. Allow your eyes to close and sit or lie quietly for several minutes. Explore the muscles in your body starting at your feet and working your way up to the top of your head. Try to become aware of any muscles or muscle groups which might be tense or

might contain reservoirs of stress. Pay close attention to the muscles of your shoulders, the back of your neck, and the muscles of your face.

STEP 2

Now take a deep breath and stretch your arms, legs and neck. Stretch out your arms and legs allowing the muscles to pull to their fullest. As you are doing this, take a deep breath and now let it out very quickly pulling your arms and legs back towards you.

STEP 3

You are going to be asked systematically to tense a specific muscle group and then hold it for at least five seconds and then relax, letting go of all the tightness in that particular muscle group.

A Word of Caution: Do not tense a muscle to the point where it is hurting you. If you have had a back injury or in the past suffered an injury to some particular muscle group, be aware of this and do not tense that particular muscle group as much as the others. You must be aware of your own limitations in tensing the muscles.

Studying the tension will become extremely important in this exercise. You must study and think about how your muscles feel when you are tensing them and then realize the difference when you allow them to "let go."

Remember, you will never get rid of absolutely all of the tension in the body. Some levels of tension are essential for maintaining attention and normal daily performance. We are attempting to get rid of any of the chronic, excessive tension which robs our body of energy and reinforces the fear reactions in our life.

STEP 4

You are now ready to begin with the exercise. You should have taken your five deep breaths, letting them out slowly and now are lying or sitting in a relaxed position. Free your mind of any extraneous thoughts because you are going to need to concentrate on the exercises. As with the other exercises in this book, it would be ideal if someone were able to record the following exercise on a tape recorder and then you could play it back during your session. If no one is available, then you could record this session yourself. Alternatively, you can read this section while you are performing the exercise.*

Important Note: The instructions for tensing should be stated in a harsher, more demanding voice, while the instructions to relax should be in a softer, more flowing tone.

RELAXATION SESSION NUMBER 1

Now it is time to begin. Allow yourself to find the most comfortable position you can. Make sure that none of your clothing is binding. If you have on a very tight wristwatch or ring, take it off. We do not want any extraneous sensations to interfere with your training procedure. Make sure that your head is supported so that it docs not rock back and forth. Now take the deep breaths, letting them out slowly while you say the number "one" silently to yourself on the exhalation. Do this about five times and on the fifth time, allow your eyes to close and let yourself sink down as much as you can into a deep state of relaxation.

Allow your thoughts to focus on your hands. Form a mental picture of your hands. Make a fist and squeezing tightly, hold the pressure for five to ten seconds. You may notice that your hand will tremble slightly; this is normal. Now let go. Let your fingers spread outward, letting all of the tension out. As you unclench your fist, you will notice that there are probably tingling sensations in your hand. This is the tension releasing from the muscle. Allow fifteen or twenty seconds to pass, with hands in the relaxed position. Study the difference between how your hand felt when you were tensing it and how it now feels while you are relaxing. Make a fist again — hold — let go. Study the difference between tension and relaxation again. Allow this feeling of relaxation to

---

*(An excellent relaxation tape, which you can write away for, is available from BMA Audio Cassettes, 270 Madison Avenue, New York, N.Y. 10016)

become very familiar. Notice how pleasing the sensation is when you "let go."

Now visualize the muscles in your upper arm, your biceps. Tense the muscles in your biceps — hold it — let go. Notice that your upper arms feel somewhat heavy and may even feel warm as you go deeper into body relaxation. Remember, when you tense one muscle group, do not tense any other ones. Try to concentrate specifically on the single muscle group with which you are working. Tense the biceps again — hold it — let go. It is as if a flow of warmth moves into your biceps as they relax. Focus now on the back of your arms, your triceps. Tense the triceps — hold it (study the tension) — let go. This time allow the muscles to relax throughout your whole arm. Allow your arms to become very loose and limp.

Now, tense all the muscles in your arms. Tense as many of the muscles as possible — hold it — let go. When you let go this time, let all the tension flow down your arms and out your finger tips. Let that tense feeling be replaced by a warm, heavy sensation.

Develop a mental image of your forehead. Create tension in your forehead by frowning — hold — let go and, as you do, notice that the tension in your forehead seems to disappear. That tense, tight feeling disappears as you let go. Picture in your mind that your forehead becomes smooth and wrinkle-free as you allow it to relax. Tense your forehead again, frowning and wrinkling up your forehead — hold it — let go, allowing all of the tension to flow out of your forehead. Your forehead is left very relaxed, feeling very smooth, and tension-free.

Now picture your face. Tighten the muscles around your nose and around your eyes — hold it — let go. When you tense the muscles around your face, be aware of the small muscles around your eyes and around your nose. Tense the central region of your face again — hold it — let go. Notice how smooth and tension-free the central part of your face feels. Visualize that the relaxation which you experienced in your forehead and central region of your face is now beginning to spread out like gently massaging fingers to all parts of your face. And as these fingers touch other parts of your face, the tension is beginning to disappear.

While you are working on your face, you should still be allowing all of the muscles in your arms to continue and maintain their deep relaxation. Now visualize your mouth and your jaw. Allow the other parts of your face to maintain relaxation and press your lips together very hard — hold it — let go. Let the relaxation rush into the areas around your lips and your jaw. Your jaw may suddenly feel heavy and you may feel the flow of warmth moving into the lower part of your face. Let the relaxation from your forehead and the central region of your face now flow down into your lips and into the muscles in your jaw. As you relax the muscles of the lower part of your face your lips will be slightly apart. Now take a minute and study the relaxation in your face. Check to see if any muscles maintain any amount of tension. If they do, tense them — hold it — and let go. Once you are satisfied that the muscles in your face are relaxed, study that relaxation, allow yourself to enjoy the achievement of facial relaxation.

Picture the area of your neck in your mind. First note whether there is any tension in your neck. Tense the muscles in your neck, the sides of your neck, and the back of your neck — hold it — let go. Notice the tension that left the back and the sides of your neck. Be aware of this very soothing contrast.

Picture the muscles in your shoulders, the tops of your shoulders, and the backs of your shoulders. Tense these muscles — hold it — let go. Study the relaxation. Tense them again — hold it — let go. All of the time the muscles in your face and your arms and neck should remain in deep relaxation.

Focus on the area of your stomach. As you take a deep breath, make the muscles in your stomach as hard as possible — hold it — let go. As the breath exhales from your lips, notice the tension that seems to flow out of your stomach. Take another deep breath, tense the muscles of your stomach and abdominal area — hold it — let go. Let a feeling of warmth move into the area of your stomach. Study the relaxation in your stomach, shoulders, neck, face and arms for several minutes.

Now picture the muscles in your thighs. Tense them — hold it — let go. Notice the difference between tension and relaxation and you will also notice that the muscles in your arms and legs will become slightly heavier as you go deeper into relaxation. This is very normal and is a sign that you are progressing very nicely with the exercise. Tense the muscles of your thighs again — hold it — let go. Study the difference between tension and relaxation in your thighs for a minute.

Now tense the muscles in your calves — hold it — let go. As you let go, you may exhale your breath, feeling all of the tension leaving your body. Notice that your thighs are still relaxed. When you tense your calf muscles, you should allow your thigh muscles to remain in their deep state of relaxation. Tense the muscles in your calves again — hold it — let go. Study the relaxation.

Tense the muscles in your legs, the thighs and calves together. Tense your leg muscles — hold it — let go. All of the other muscles which we have worked with should maintain the relaxation while you tense the muscles in your legs. Tense the muscles in the legs again — hold it — let go. Study and enjoy the relaxation.

Now tighten the muscles in your feet, turn your toes downward as if you were trying to make a fist — hold it — let go. Study the relaxation, and notice the difference between tension and relaxation in the muscles of your toes and your feet. Maintain relaxation in your calves and thighs while you are working with your feet. Now try it again, tense the muscles in your toes and feet — hold it — let go.

It is now time to check for any areas of tension within your body. Start at your toes while you are maintaining a deep relaxation and run a check up your body through all of the muscles with which we have worked. If during your check you find that any muscle group seems to be holding on to any tension, tense that muscle group — hold it — let go. You may have to do this for some muscle groups which have been tense for a long, long time. While you are relaxing, remember that your lips should be slightly parted and you should maintain that smooth sensation over the muscles in your face. Your breathing should be deep and regular. Allow a warm, heavy sensation to flow through your body as if this current of relaxation were traveling throughout every single muscle in your body.

Spend four or five minutes in the position you are in now, allowing the relaxation to deepen and to become more and more pleasing. Notice how much better you feel when you are relaxed. Focus all your attention on the joys and excitement of deep relaxation.

When you want to stop the exercise, simply flex your arms, flex your legs, take a deep breath, and open your eyes. Remember to sit up slowly, allowing yourself to stretch, and see if you can maintain the relaxation for as long as possible even when you have finished the exercise.

It is very important to try and maintain any carry-over effect from the exercises. If you are able to maintain a relaxed feeling for two minutes after the first time you do one of the exercises, this is good. The next time try to make it four minutes, then five, and gradually you will be substituting relaxation for tension in your daily activities.

TRAINING REGIMEN

Next in your training program will be to learn the autogenic training exercises. These exercises are to be performed a minimum of three times daily for 10 to 15 minutes. You should not practice for more than 15 minutes each time. The exercises may be practiced more than three times daily, but it is not recommended that they be done more than five times during the course of one 24-hour period.

Each practice session will be begun and ended in the exact same manner.

INITIATING THE AUTOGENIC TRAINING

Assume the autogenic training position and proceed by checking each of your major muscle systems. If you notice that any of them are particularly tight, allow them to become loose, limp and slack. Take a deep breath, let it out slowly and close your eyes. At this point, you are ready to begin the autogenic exercises.

It will help considerably, if while silently repeating the exercises to yourself, you visualize the specific part of the body you are dealing with.

PRACTICING THE EXERCISES

There are two methods which can be employed in practicing the autogenic exercises.

1. The first is to practice the exercises in a room which provides you enough light, so that you will be able to read the phrases. Put yourself in the autogenic position and open your eyes to read the first phrase —

My right arm is heavy

Once you have read this phrase, close your eyes and assume the autogenic position. Repeat this phrase silently to yourself ten times. Open your eyes and read the next phrase —

My left arm is heavy

Close your eyes and repeat ten times.

Repeat this procedure for each one of the phrases until the ten to fifteen minute time period is up.

My arms are heavy
My right leg is heavy
My left leg is heavy
My legs are heavy
My arms and legs are heavy
My right arm is warm
My left arm is warm
My arms are warm
My right leg is warm
My left leg is warm
My legs are warm
My arms and legs are warm
My arms and legs are heavy and warm
My heartbeat is calm and regular
My breathing is calm and regular
My stomach is warm

My forehead is cool
I am calm and relaxed
The muscles in my arms and legs are loose, limp and slack

After just a few sessions, you should be able to repeat the complete autogenic formula without having to read it. This is a goal which you should try to attain as soon as possible.

2. The second method which you may use is to have someone you know or you yourself record the phrases on a cassette tape recorder. Allow enough time for the ten to fifteen minute session. State the phrase into the tape recorder and allow a space for mental repetition. As with the first method, after a very short period of time, you should be able to complete the formula from memory.

A helpful hint is to write down the autogenic formula which you are going to practice on a piece of paper and look at it numerous times during the day. This will help commit the phrases to memory.

It is essential that the phrases be memorized so that they can be repeated mentally at any time or place.

The use of autogenics for systematic phobic reduction does not require any special ability at memorization. Throughout my experience with patients, I have found that committing the phrases to memory takes very little time and can be accomplished quite readily with practice.

TERMINATING THE EXERCISES

All of the exercise sessions are to be terminated in the exact same manner. You are to say to yourself, time to terminate this exercise. You will immediately flex your arms, flex your legs, take a deep breath and open your eyes.

Under no circumstances should you immediately jump up. This would cause your body to go into hypotension, or a state of low blood pressure, and may cause some dizziness and possible fainting. After the exercise has been terminated, you should spend a few moments moving your arms and legs and then get up in a normal fashion.

Remember, all of these exercises may be practiced at any time during the day and night. The one important rule is that you should always begin and terminate the exercise in the exact same manner.

Once you have become proficient at using the autogenic exercises, then you will be able to switch on the autogenic state in a matter of minutes. In fact, many of my patients report that once they have become proficient at using the exercises, the simple step of taking a deep breath and letting it out slowly, immediately activates all the autogenic processes within the body.

It is extremely important for you to remember always that the autogenic exercises within themselves will not rid you of your fear. These exercises need to be combined with the desensitization process. But in order for desensitization to be effective, you must first gain the ability to relax at will. The autogenics must be practiced on a daily basis in order to maintain your efficiency. This is not a method which you can try once and then forget about. In order for the autogenic state to replace your fear and anxiety reaction when faced with the phobic situation, object or thought, you must be able to adopt this procedure without thinking about it.

PASSIVE CONCENTRATION

Once you know the basics of autogenic training, developing the proper method to use these training exercises is most important. Passive concentration will serve as your key in the development of adequate mastery of autogenic training.

Each one of us is caught up in the day-to-day strivings of today's society. Make more money, get a bigger house, have a nicer car, get your children a better education, all are parts of the burden which society has placed upon us. Several times a day, we make decisions as to whether we're going to pursue our own goals or those set by society for us. This active choice habitually occurs during our daily activities and is characterized by various degrees of attention in combination with the use of energy towards goal-directed activities. These goal-directed activities and constant strivings are what Hans Selye has commented on in his numerous books and articles regarding the worldwide stress epidemic as the cause of many stress-related disorders, such as ulcers, headaches and nervous tics.

Since early childhood, we have been taught that there are only "winners" and "losers." There is no middle ground — you either win or lose. The fear of failure becomes such an all-pervasive fact of life that we are not fully aware of the implications of this fear-inducing behavior. We therefore use active concentration or goal-oriented activity through most of our youth and adult lives to satisfy our wants and to quell our fear of failure.

An example of active goal-seeking behavior is seen in Elliott Roberts, a 36-year-old banking executive, who had set his sights on achieving the rank of Assistant Vice-President of a large banking system. All his activities were directed towards this end, and his behavior was fashioned to ensure his eventual promotion to this job position. His relationship with his wife and children suffered over a period of four years and his level of anxiety and fear of failure continued to increase. Many of the symptoms of a chronic phobic reaction began to show up in this 36-year-old man, who was quickly burning himself out. Several ulcers and episodes of colitis were not enough to convince him that his active goal-directed behavior might eventually contribute to his downfall.

He constantly told his wife: "I've got to get that job. Once I get the job I'll be happy and we can all relax and begin living life again."

Well, he got the job and what do you think happened afterwards?

If you guessed that he immediately set his sights on the next position up the ladder and immediately started behaving in the same manner as before, then you are right. The gradual disintegration of his physical, emotional, and family life did little to convince him that his active goal-seeking behavior was, in very real terms, counterproductive.

If we were to examine his total life structure, we would find that this active concentration on goal-directed behaviors exemplified all of his activities. Even when on the golf course, this individual would constantly try to hit the ball farther than anyone else. Eight out of ten times the ball would either slice or hook. Usually at the second or third attempt to get a straight drive, he would finally relax, take an attitude of, "If I hit it, I hit it," and then, with all his muscles working in coordination and with a nice relaxed easy swing, he would hit the ball much farther than on any of his other tries.

I am not suggesting that people should not have goal-directed activities, and should not seek to better themselves intellectually and materially. What I am against is the use of active concentration to obtain these ends. By contrast, the use of *passive* goal-seeking behaviors would result in a decrease in phobic related diseases (stress, anxiety) and would still allow people to meet their goals, without destroying their lives in the process.

Passive concentration is the key which will unlock the doors to the successful use of autogenic training, desensitization, and eventually the reduction and extinction of your phobic reactions.

The whole secret to passive concentration is to "let it happen." In active relaxation, you are "trying" to initiate some response. The act of trying in and of itself will tense the muscles and cause a tension response, similar to that of a phobic response. The individual who makes excessive efforts will automatically preclude his getting the required results from the training session.

The harder you try, the less results you achieve. This is known by many scientists as the "principal of paradoxical intentions."

Dr. Schultz felt that the key to obtaining the autogenic state was to yield to passivity and permit yourself to slip into the autogenic training position.

PASSIVE RELAXATION

Passive concentration on the autogenic training exercises consists of the following:

(a) Mentally repeat the specific autogenic formula silently to yourself.

(b) Develop a mental image of the specific area of the body which you are dealing with through the autogenic training formula.

(c) Maintain a consistent and timed repetition of the formula.

(d) Properly time shift from one formula to the next.

(e) Properly interspace the desensitization hierarchy. (see Ch. 6)

The mental process of "passive relaxation" is based upon the subject using a casual, relaxed attitude which involves only a minimal use of goal-directed striving.

Possibly one of the best ways to illustrate the use of passive concentration as opposed to active concentration will be through the following examples. Think back to a time, early in your childhood, when you were caught up in a fantasy of chasing butterflies. Picture a lush green lawn dotted with trees and flowers. A small yellow butterfly dances, tantalizingly close to your fingertips as you chase after it. The harder you chase, the more you strive towards catching that butterfly, the less your effort is rewarded. The butterfly keeps dancing on the wind, just eluding the outstretched grasp. Finally, in frustration and dejection, you sit on the lawn and give up chasing the butterfly. But lo and behold, the butterfly flits towards you and eventually lands on your shoulder.

This example illustrates the fact that the harder you strive towards something the less your efforts will be rewarded. But finally when you relax and allow the body to activate its own self-regulatory (relaxation) mechanisms, then passive relaxation will allow you to program your body responses to phobia and fear reactions.

Sandy is another example of a person who needed to relax in order to apply autogenic training and desensitization successfully. She was referred to me by a local oncologist who maintained a large practice dealing specifically with cancerous tumors.

The doctor was quite concerned because, as he reviewed her

file, it was evident that she had visited five physicians before arriving at his office for evaluation. Her major complaint was "stomach pain." Medical tests were run to check for the possibility of any other type of organic involvement of the stomach or intestine. All tests proved negative. X-ray examination of the area also proved negative, not only for any type of ulcer, but for any cancerous tumor. The physician reported to me that all results of his tests were negative and, in fact, he did not try to duplicate some of the previous tests. From the information in her file, he realized that several tests had been run within a very short period of time with the same negative results. Her history showed that three close relatives had died within the past seven years of cancer.

I accepted the referral and saw her in my office for evaluation. During the course of the evaluation, she was somewhat resistant to my questioning. It was quite obvious that she was upset at being referred to a "shrink." She assured me over and over again that she was not crazy and that her pain was being caused by cancer.

I spent a considerable amount of time going through the patient's file with her and found upon examining her medical records, that she had been evaluated at the Mayo Clinic. All their results were negative also and the diagnosis had been a phobic reaction towards cancer. I went over this report with her and she was surprised at the comment. Evidently, none of the other physicians had explained fully the results of her Mayo Clinic examination. The doctors at Mayo further felt that much of her stomach pain was brought about by severe anxiety. I diagrammed the situation on the blackboard and showed her how she had been caught up in the vicious circle of fear reactions. The more she tried to avoid thinking about the cancer, the greater the anxiety became. Her obsessional thoughts about the family's past history of cancer were causing her to remain in a chronic state of fear. Although the stomach pain and nausea were diagnosed as being from her anxiety, any time these symptoms appeared, they reinforced her belief that death was "just around the corner."

Several sessions passed before Sandy was able to accept my explanation, substantiated by numerous physicians, as to the cause of her pain. The deeper we explored her reactions, the more evident it became that she was involved in a very severe chronic phobic situation. I had her fill out a fear identity and intensity form and a severe phobic reaction towards disease showed up as her most prominent fear.

I explained to her that there was a need to rid herself of the fear of cancer. She did not have cancer at the present time, but her constant state of heightened anxiety could possible cause ulcers and other physical harm if the phobia was not reduced significantly.

She appeared to be somewhat reluctant to begin the program and we spent a little bit more time talking about the need for reducing her fear.

Sandy finished the forms and we developed a hierarchy of her fear together. Normally, the patient would develop the hierarchy and then allow me to check it over for any possible problem areas. In this case, we did the hierarchy together since I felt her commitment towards therapy was not as great as it should be. After developing the hierarchy, she began the relaxation-autogenic training. Again, she was somewhat resistant to begin this type of therapy and we had to work very hard to increase her level of motivation towards taking the responsibility for getting rid of her fear reaction.

The reluctance for therapy in this case is not unusual. Sometimes, with patients who fear a disease process for which no medical cause can be found, there is a dependency upon the fear reaction. They become adjusted to other people's reactions towards them and may even tend to manipulate the situation towards a secondary gain. We can describe secondary gain as a method of behavior in which the individual is receiving some "pay-off" for being ill. Sandy was receiving secondary gain in the form of a response from her husband. Since she had developed her "disease," her husband had taken over most of the household chores while maintaining his full-time employment.

Unconsciously, she was developing a pattern of reaction that would make it imperative for her to maintain her "sick status." Combine these two factors together and we have a patient who, on the one hand desires to get better, and on the other fears a readjustment if it is found that her disease does not have an organic basis.

Several weeks passed, during which the patient developed the needed competency for the relaxation-autogenics. When I felt she had attained a sufficient level of control over her relaxation process, I then instructed her to begin working with the hierarchy.

One week later she was seen in follow-up treatment. During follow-up treatment, I try not to interfere with the self-help process, but in cases like Sandy's I recheck the patient on a weekly basis to make sure that he is progressing in a beneficial direction.

Upon entering my office, her first comment summarized the change in her behavior. "I can't believe it. I can't believe it. I haven't had any stomach pain for four days now." She was jumping up and down as she related these feelings to me. I calmed her down and asked her to explain further what was happening.

"I did just like you said," she began. "The first couple of days I didn't think it was going to work and I was going to quit. Nothing seemed to be working. I wasn't getting any of the feelings that you were telling me about on the tape and I was getting really discouraged. I was ready to call you and tell you that the whole thing was a lot of garbage, but my husband wanted me to try it for one more day. That morning I started the exercises as usual, but this time I really didn't care whether they worked or not. Immediately I felt my legs get very warm and I got this feeling of relaxation all over. It was the strangest thing that ever happened to me. From that point until today, I haven't had any more stomach pain. I am up to step number nine on the hierarchy, but I don't think I even really need to finish it."

I immediately told her that she did need to finish the hierarchy and that although she had achieved a good level of success in the beginning, it was imperative that she follow through with the process to its completion. She listened carefully while I explained that it would take considerably longer for her to develop the relaxation response as a habit. She was also amazed to learn that the reason for her success the last day was that she finally took a passive attitude, instead of an active one, and the exercises were then able to work effectively.

Four weeks later Sandy had completed the hierarchy and no recurring symptoms of her stomach problem were found. She fully realized the need to continue practicing the self-desensitization process towards her cancerophobia. When she was not working on this specific phobia, she could apply the relaxation process to any other fears which she had now or which might arise in the future.

Not all cases concerning a disease phobia are resolved as quickly at Sandy's. Phobias towards disease are usually quite complicated and the patient must learn to continue practicing, even if the results are not immediately forthcoming. Discouragement will be the main enemy to this type of individual, and as with Sandy, they usually are trying too hard to accomplish the relaxation autogenic process. The harder they try to accomplish this goal, the fewer results they get. Finally when they are able to approach the situation using passive concentration, they obtain the needed physical responses for completion of the desensitization process.

Although cases like Sandy's are difficult to cure, I have seen good results obtained by others using the self-treatment program. It should be cautioned at this point that this program for desensitization of disease phobia should not be attempted unless you receive clearance from your physician. This process should never be used for reduction of a disease phobia without receiving a thorough medical check-up first to eliminate an organic cause for symptoms.

WHAT IF MY THOUGHTS ARE INTERRUPTED?

As you begin doing the autogenic exercises, you may notice that your train of thought will be occasionally interrupted. When this happens, do not despair. Very gently and calmly bring your conscious thought back to the training exercise.

Treat this process as if you were gently cupping a delicate butterfly in your hands. If you act too quickly and apply too much effort, the butterfly will be damaged. This analogy also applies to training your mind to perform the exercise process.

A phrase which has been extremely helpful to my patients is: *"My thoughts are calm and clear."* It can be inserted into the repetition process when you notice that there is a break in your thought process, and should be repeated silently to yourself three times. At that point you will be ready to resume the autogenic exercises.

During the initial phases of your training, it will not be un-common for you to have to use this method of re-training your thought process numerous times. Learning the desired skill of maintaining a consistent train of thought during the exercise process will develop as you progress through the practice sessions.

For those of you who are not quite clear as to the effect that thought distraction can have on your practice sessions, let me take a moment to cite the following example.

Debbie was beginning her third week of practicing the relaxation-autogenic therapy. She was just starting to construct the initial phase of the hierarchy and had been obtaining good results during the practice sessions. She started her mid-day session after the children returned to school following lunch. She was five minutes into the session when a car backfired outside her house. The noise immediately came into her conscious thought process and the chaining began as follows:

She hears the car backfire . . . she thinks about her car sitting in the driveway . . . she wonders if the noise in the engine means that something is broken . . . she thinks about the expense of repairing the car . . . she thinks about the raise her husband should have received last month . . . she thinks about the increased cost of groceries . . . the two children will need new shoes next month and that will cost money.

It can easily be seen from the above example that the simple noise of a car backfiring had become the precipitating event in a chain of disruptive thoughts. If she had not stopped this chaining effect, it would have continued and in a matter of minutes her practice session could have been severely disrupted.

Once the chaining effect begins, the harder you attempt to use active concentration in order to stabilize your thought process, the less positive results you will have. Once again, you must use passive concentration, mentally shrug your shoulders at the disruption and silently repeat the phrase: *"My thoughts are calm and clear."*

Do this three times and then begin again where you left off in your training process.

Just like everything else, the ability to stop disruptive thought chaining will take time to develop. Be patient; everyone can learn to do it with practice.

CHAPTER SIX
How to Use Systematic Desensitization

"The free man is he who does not fear
to go to the end of his thought."
LEON BLUM

Systematic desensitization refers to a highly structured program by which you gradually become insensitive or non-reactive to whatever stimulus has been causing your fear reaction. This method of therapy did not come about by accident, but was the outcome of many years of intensive behavioral research.

Dr. Joseph Wolpe, a psychiatrist, began work in the late 1950's on a method which combined psychotherapy with some of the principles of Jacobson's relaxation technique. Wolpe programmed his relaxation training to be completed in about six interviews. He instructed patients to practice at home for two 15-minute periods a day. As an outcome of his research into relaxation training, Wolpe (1958) developed a form of counterconditioning which he called systematic desensitization.

After many years of research, Wolpe found that the autonomically controlled body reactions that accompany relaxation are diametrically opposed to those characteristic of anxiety. Through animal experimentation, he found that it was possible to overcome a pattern of behavior by replacing it with an antagonistic pattern of behavior in the same situation. He further proposed that; "If a response inhibitory of anxiety can be made to occur in the presence of the anxiety-provoking stimuli, it will weaken the bond between these stimuli and the anxiety."

Wolpe felt that one of the keys to anxiety reduction is training in relaxation. Relaxation therefore becomes the antagonistic response to anxiety and the basis for systematic desensitization. Wolpe further reasoned that muscle relaxation is physically incompatible with changes brought about during the anxiety response. In other words, it is impossible to be both "anxious" and "relaxed" at the same time.

Almost invariably, relaxation methods bring about at least a temporary release of tension and leave the patient feeling much better. But the real test of anxiety and fear reduction through relaxation techniques has come with research involving phobias.

Larson (1966) performed experiments dealing with different approaches to snake-phobic behavior. Two groups were told to imagine frightening experiences involving snakes. One group was told to remain calm and relaxed during the experiment and the other was instructed to relive their experience of fear to the fullest extent. A third group was hypnotized and given a post-hypnotic suggestion that they would no longer be afraid of snakes. After the experiment, all three groups showed significantly less fear of snakes, but the group that was instructed to relax maintained these good results for a much longer period. Relaxation training for the reduction of anxiety appears to have a longer lasting effect than the other therapies tried.

Because many of our anxieties are conditioned responses, there are several steps we can take to "decondition" these reactions. You should always remember that conditioned reactions are very similar to reflexes, but the general scientific feeling is that they are learned and not inherited.

Because they are automatic or reflexive in nature, it is very difficult to discuss many of these problems with people who are experiencing the reaction at that particular moment. Many people are not fully aware of the conditioned (reflex) action of their fears and phobias. This may readily explain why people can tell themselves repeatedly that a particular stimulus or situation is not going to cause them to become upset and yet, when presented with that situation either physically or through their imagination, they display the same reactions over and over again.

Unless something is done to counteract this conditioned response, the response may generalize and spread to other areas of the person's behavior. Fears can cause a chain reaction just as a car stopping suddenly will cause others to pile up behind it.

An example of this chain reaction can be seen in Jane, who was approached by a stranger on the way to school when she was only nine years old. The stranger made an attempt to force her into the car, but she resisted and ran away. For two years after the incident, Jane displayed extreme anxiety and avoidance behavior whenever she met strange or unknown men. This reaction was evident even in her parents' company. In one instance, she walked into the classroom to find a male substitute teacher. Her reaction was immediate. Upon seeing the man, she turned and ran from the room screaming. She was seen for prolonged psychotherapy and eventually her fear of strangers seemed to disappear.

I saw her when she was twenty-three years old and she reported that she still became extremely nervous around any men, turning down dates with co-workers just because she was scared to go out with them. She couldn't understand why this happened.

I asked her to describe in greater detail other instances in which she experienced apprehension and fear when near men.

She thought for a moment and then began to list them as follows:

1. Being in an elevator and having a man enter.
2. Taking notes into any man's office.
3. Going out on dates.
4. Seeing a man walking towards her on the street.
5. Riding the subway with men around her.

It was quite evident to me that this woman was suffering from a generalization of her phobia towards men, which she developed as a very young girl. Initially, everyone believed that she had recovered from the frightening incident when she was nine years old. However, her fear of men had simply been suppressed until she took a new job. On this new job, she was more unsure of herself and thus became susceptible to the previous phobic conditioning towards meeting men.

Many times during an illness or when someone is under stress, there is an increase or rebirth of long-buried phobias. When a phobia recurs, this means that it has not been resolved satisfactorily in the past and has simply been covered up, only to reappear when the body or emotions become susceptible.

Once the complete extent of her phobia was discovered, Jane participated in the systematic desensitization program and at last report was making excellent progress at overcoming this phobia which was long overdue to be extinguished.

SYSTEMATIC DESENSITIZATION

The basics of systematic desensitization can be broken into three distinct sets of operations, all of which are interrelated. The individual must first correctly identify his phobia using the identification forms in Chapter 4. He is then trained in the techniques of relaxation. In the past, the usual method for this procedure was the use of Dr. Jacobson's progressive relaxation method. This method has been found to be effective but I feel that autogenic therapy provides a quicker form of success for the patient. In order to fully practice progressive relaxation, one must devote a considerable amount of time to the procedure itself. The opposite is true of autogenic training; when one becomes proficient at the technique, it may take only a few minutes to fully activate the relaxation technique. There is another distinct advantage to autogenics in that while progressive relaxation must be done either sitting or lying down, in the advanced forms, autogenic training can be practiced with eyes open, standing, walking and even while working. Therefore, autogenic training allows you to practice your antagonistic response to fear throughout the day.

Once the individual has learned to relax he is then taught to practice relaxation while imagining the various stages of his fear response. This is done by means of a hierarchy or graduated list of fear-producing situations.

The standard hierarchy is a written list of events, designed to elicit the same response as the real life experience. The list of items on the hierarchy numbers 15, since I have found that too few items on a hierarchy can be just as troublesome as too many items.

Since you will be creating your own hierarchy, it will meet your specific needs. However, since some phobias are found consistently in a large number of people, I will give you examples of several hierarchies which you can use as is, if you have that specific phobic reaction, or which you may adapt to your own particular situation.

If you are not going to use one of the standard hierarchies listed, then your first step after identifying your phobia is to sit down in a nice quiet place and, using the other phobia hierarchies as a guide, list on separate index cards the various stages of your phobic reaction. Card number 15 should be the actual phobic situation itself and will be the most fearful and anxiety-producing.

Your descriptions on these cards should be short and very clear-cut. Try to be as specific as possible. If you are too general, then the scene to be imagined from the card will not produce a sufficient fear response. We are trying to duplicate the actual build-up of a phobic reaction.

Once the 15 cards have been written, then you are to stack them in order of the increasing anxiety they produce in you. The least anxiety-producing statement will be on the top, with the most anxiety-producing statement on the bottom.

If your forms in Chapter 4 have identified more than one phobia, there may be several stacks of cards.

I should caution that only one phobic reaction should be worked through at a time.

Most people find that after working through one phobic reaction, it becomes much simpler to use this process on any subsequent fears.

After you have constructed the hierarchy on the index cards, then check it over and compare it to the hierarchies in this book. There may be ways in which you can simplify your own hierarchy by following the examples.

If your hierarchy is one that has been listed in the book, then you should copy each one of the statements down on the index cards, exactly as if you were developing the hierarchy yourself. Then go through the index cards and if you find that any statement needs to be changed for your particular situation, then do so at this time. Please feel free to make any modifications in the standard hierarchies so that they will be personalized for your own use. The hierarchies in this book are only to be used as a guide and should be modified to be more useful in your specific situation.

Take some time now to look through these samples of hierarchies.

FLYING PHOBIA HIERARCHY
1. You are looking at a magazine and see pictures of airplanes.
2. You are watching television and see a commercial about flying.
3. You are at the movies or watching television and the topic is airplanes.
4. You hear the sound of an airplane flying over you.
5. You find out that you're going to be taking a trip by airplane.
6. You see yourself packing for that trip by airplane.
7. You are driving towards the airport.
8. You are entering the parking area for the airport and see planes taking off and landing.
9. You enter the airport terminal and check your luggage.
10. You are waiting to board the airplane and see all the other passengers.
11. Now you are seated in the airplane and are looking around at the other people and the inside of the aircraft.

12. The airplane begins to taxi down the runway and you feel the vibrations and hear the sounds of the engines.
13. The aircraft is rolling down the runway very fast and picking up speed. The engine noise and vibrations are increasing.
14. The front wheel of the airplane lifts off the ground and you feel the pull of gravity as the plane breaks free of the runway. You are now climbing high into the sky.
15. The plane levels out and is now flying at a high altitude. There are constant vibrations and small bumps as the airplane continues its flight. You look out the window to see how high you are.

HIERARCHY FOR FEAR OF NIGHT

1. You see the word "night" written in large black letters on a piece of paper.
2. A friend tells you it is going to be a dark night.
3. You look out your window and notice that the sun is beginning to set.
4. You are told you are going to be alone in the house this evening.
5. The sun continues to go down and it is gradually getting darker.
6. The street lights go on as it darkens.
7. The cars that drive by have their headlights on.
8. You have to turn on the lights in your house because it is becoming dark.
9. You look out the window and can barely see any of the objects around your house.
10. The streets lights are on.
11. As you look out the window in the middle of the night, everything is hidden by darkness.
12. It is 2 o'clock in the morning and there are sounds of insects outside your house in the darkness, as you stand by the window.
13. You open up your door and begin to step into the darkness.

14. You are outside your house and it is dark around you, except for the light coming from the open door.
15. The door closes behind you and you remain in complete darkness outside your house. You stand there for about five minutes.

HIERARCHY FOR FEAR OF INJECTIONS
1. Someone mentions the word "needle" to you.
2. Someone is telling you they received an injection last week.
3. There is a picture of a hypodermic needle in a magazine.
4. You are watching a doctor prepare an injection.
5. The doctor inserts the needle into the flask and draws the fluid into the syringe.
6. The doctor walks up to a patient and readies for the injection into the patient's arm.
7. The needle is pushed into the skin and the fluid is injected.
8. The doctor tells you that you are going to have an injection.
9. You go to the doctor's office and are sitting in the waiting room, waiting for your injection.
10. The nurse calls your name and indicates you are next.
11. Once in the doctor's office, you see him preparing the syringe for the injection.
12. You see the needle is about 1½ inches long, silver and very shiny.
13. The doctor comes over and takes your left arm and rolls up your sleeve. He applies alcohol to the spot where the injection is going to be.
14. You feel the needle piercing your skin.
15. There is a burning sensation as the fluid is injected into your arm.

HIERARCHY FOR A FEAR OF SLEEP
1. You are watching television and see a commercial for beds.
2. The commercial talks about people who have problems sleeping and shows several people after a restful night's sleep.

3. Several people come up to you and ask you if you have had a good night's sleep.

4. It is getting late in the day and you begin thinking about going to bed at night.

5. You look outside the window and it is dark.

6. A member of your family mentions to you that it is almost time to go to bed.

7. You walk into your bedroom and look down at your bed.

8. You turn off the lights around the house as you prepare for bed.

9. You walk over to the bed and stand looking at it.

10. You sit down at the edge of the bed and turn out the light.

11. The room is completely dark as you put your head down on the pillow.

12. Once under the sheets, you look around into the darkness of the room.

13. You close your eyes and breathe in and out, deep and slow.

14. You lie there with your eyes closed, listening for sounds in the room.

15. The room is quiet, your eyes are closed and your breathing is deep and regular. You are going to sleep . . . you are asleep.

HIERARCHY FOR SPEAKING IN FRONT OF A GROUP

1. You have just been informed that you're going to have to make a speech in front of 50 people.

2. You are going over your notes for the speech and picture the people watching and listening to you.

3. You are practicing your speech in front of a mirror.

4. You are in the car driving to the place where you're going to be giving the speech.

5. You are rehearsing the speech in your mind as you drive.

6. You park the car and enter the building where you're going to be giving the speech.

7. You go to the room where the speech is to be given and look out at the empty seats.

8. You are going over some of the notes for the speech as the room begins to fill with people.

9. You are sitting up in front of the people and look out at all their faces as they look in your direction.

10. You are standing up to give the speech and looking out at the people's faces.

11. You have been introduced for the speech and the microphone is in front of you.

12. The room becomes very quiet as everyone waits for you to begin the speech.

13. You look down at your notes and begin talking.

14. There is a point during the speech when you lose your train of thought and begin to panic slightly, but you regain your composure and continue.

15. The room is absolutely quiet as you speak and everyone's eyes are on you. It is obvious that each person is listening to every word you say.

HIERARCHY FOR FEAR OF HEIGHTS

1. There is a ladder raised against the side of a building. You look at the ladder and then let your eyes travel up the side of the building.

2. You walk over to the ladder and put your foot on the first rung. Then you put both feet on the first rung, holding the sides of the ladder with your hands. You stand there for a few moments and then proceed up to the next rung.

3. You are now halfway up the ladder and look up towards the top.

4. You climb a little bit higher and then look down. You focus on the ground and look to your right and then to your left.

5. You are standing outside a very tall building and slowly look up all the way to the top.

6. You are entering the building and stepping into the elevator.

7. The elevator carries you to the upper floors of the building. You are now at the 15th floor and you leave the elevator.

8. You walk over towards one of the building's windows. As you get closer to the window you can see the sides and tops of many other buildings.

9. You are at the window and look out and down. Below you the people, cars and sidewalks look very, very small.

10. You are in a room and there is a balcony outside a large glass door. This balcony is six stories above the ground and you can see this by looking out the glass doors.

11. You open the glass doors and walk out onto the balcony. All around you is open sky and you walk towards the railing which surrounds the balcony.

12. Placing both hands on the railing, you lean your head over slightly and look down towards the ground.

13. You step back from the railing and then step forward again, placing your hands on the railing and looking over towards the ground.

14. You again step back from the balcony, wait a few seconds and then return to the balcony, to look over again.

15. This time when you look over the balcony you do not put your hands on the railing, but standing back from the edge, lean your head over slightly to look down.

IN VIVO DESENSITIZATION

I have found in my practice that it is very helpful to have the patient experience a portion of the fear-evoking stimulus in a real life or "in vivo" situation after they have completed the desensitization program using the standard or written hierarchy. Of course, this can only apply to stimuli which are of a physical nature. The in vivo experience tends to accelerate the desensitization process.

I have tried to restrict the use of in vivo desensitization to patients who have already completed the regular desensitization program through the use of imagery. Less than 8% of my patients have been unable to use their imagination for the hierarchy process. If hypnosis does not work, then I may give them a very mild trial of in vivo desensitization. But I must emphasize that for me, in vivo desensitization has been most useful as a follow-up or bridging technique after the normal desensitization process.

By bridging technique, I mean it provides a tool for the patient to transfer the learning accomplished through the standard desensitization process to a real life situation. As with the desensitization process, the in vivo procedure must be used in a graduated form. Let's say the patient has been desensitized towards airplanes. The in vivo process should then be developed from a hierarchy before the patient eventually takes an airplane flight.

Mitch was very fearful of flying in airplanes. He went through the desensitization process and was quite successful, using mental imagery, at recreating trips taken in an airplane. After some practice, he was able to go through an imaginary airplane flight without the upset stomach, nervousness and other physical manifestations associated with his fear of flying. I felt that Mitch was making excellent progress, but needed the bridging technique of real life rehearsal, to complete his reduction of the fear response towards flying.

A week after he completed the desensitization program, he was required to take a business trip out of town. We felt this would be an excellent opportunity to practice real life rehearsal. Using the flying phobia hierarchy, found in this chapter, Mitch followed through the steps which he had imagined, but this time it was in a real life situation. Anytime he felt anxiety welling up inside him, he would break the bond by practicing his relaxation procedures. By not allowing panic and fear to overwhelm him, Mitch was able to complete the round trip flight with only a minimal amount of physical discomfort. He reported the flight back was much easier than the outgoing trip. Two weeks later he went on another flight and his symptoms continued to lessen.

By using the initial desensitization technique and then following through with a real life rehearsal, Mitch is now able to fly quite comfortably and fear of flying no longer interferes with his business.

Many patients will take the hierarchy that was used in the normal desensitization process and simply follow it through in a real life situation. Throughout the time that the in vivo process is being practiced, the patient should be performing the paired relaxation-autogenic responses to inhibit any anxiety which might occur. If the person has effectively proceeded through the standard desensitization process, then following up with the in vivo procedure should not present any serious problems. If any step in the hierarchy produces fear when tested in an in vivo situation, then the patient must go back to the normal desensitization process and rework that step in the hierarchy.

Using in vivo desensitization can be an excellent check to find out how effective your desensitization training has been. I should caution you at this time that in vivo desensitization should not be used as a short cut method, but should only be used after you have progressed through the standard desensitization exercises. If you try the in vivo desensitization without the proper pre-training, you may find that your anxiety and fear increase rather than decrease.

Prepare well in advance and make sure you have a thorough understanding of the intent and desired outcome of the process. Be consistent, don't try to change boats in mid-stream. Inconsistent, stop-and-start methods will only prolong the therapy process and may lead to needless discouragement.

Treat each one of the procedures as if your emotional and physical well-being depended on it. It may!

Wolpe (1961) reported that less than two percent of 249 patients who were followed after therapy showed a relapse.

The above statistics show that this therapy method is quite effective and most importantly, continues to be effective over a long period of time. The work of many behavior therapists with phobic patients reaffirms Dr. Wolpe's findings for this exciting method of treatment.

It is important to remember that at the heart of systematic desensitization is a technique developed by Pavlov to extinguish responses which have been conditioned to certain fear stimuli.

By progressive steps you can gradually work through your entire phobic reaction using your autogenic training to relax as you progress through the hierarchy. The length of treatment will depend upon the amount of practice you need in autogenic training and how carefully you construct the anxiety hierarchy.

Remember, it may have taken many years to develop your phobic reactions and no therapy is going to rid you of your fear overnight. You must take your time and follow the instructions carefully and accurately. If this is done then there is little doubt that you can conquer many of your acute and chronic phobic reactions.

Scientific evaluation of the procedures involved in this book are continuing all the time. Dr. Gordon L. Paul of the University of Illinois has studied extensively the effects of systematic desensitization as compared to other standard forms of therapy. His experiments were conducted with college students who displayed an acute phobic reaction towards speaking in public. Each of the students using the systematic desensitization approach constructed a hierarchy and, with relaxation, proceeded through each one of the items on the list. They soon were able to relax while proceeding through each item listed. Of the students using systematic desensitization, one hundred percent showed improvement. Only 73 percent of the next most successful treatment — hypnosis — improved. To quote Paul directly:

"The findings were overwhelmingly positive. For the first time in the history of psychological treatments a specific treatment package reliably produced measurable benefits for clients across a broad range of distressing problems in which anxiety was of fundamental importance. Relapse and 'symptom substitution' were notably lacking."

In the next chapters, we are going to be helping you set up your program. Your excitement should be building, because at this point you are getting very close to beginning your personal phobia reduction program. Your freedom from fear is just around the corner.

CHAPTER SEVEN
Setting Up Your Own Program

*"Fear is the main source of superstition,
and one of the main sources of cruelty.
To conquer fear is the beginning of
wisdom, in the pursuit of truth as in
the endeavor after a worthy manner
of life."*

BERTRAND RUSSELL:
"An Outline of Intellectual Rubbish"

Now it's time for you to set up your own program. You have read about how phobias develop, the effects of fear and how fear can disrupt your life. You have also seen how many people have worked and overcome their fears.

Patients of mine will often express a desire to resolve some emotional problem which may entail reducing a fear response. Our sessions usually begin with a thorough discussion of the circumstances under which the fear response developed, and the way in which fear is reinforced and maintained.

I then tell the patient that he must make a very serious and important decision. I usually let the words sink in, allowing them to gain their full impact:

"Will you give me a commitment right now that you will work at resolving your phobic reaction? Will you keep working at the program even if it requires you to change your lifestyle?"

If the answer is yes, then I immediately follow it with the third question. "Are you ready to take responsibility for full participation in this therapeutic endeavor?"

THE BEHAVIORAL CONTRACT — THE FIRST STEP

If the patient is committed to following the phobia reduction program, I then have him sign a behavioral contract (sample below). This contract serves to reinforce the patient's commitment to practice the therapeutic methods every day. It also helps remind him that he will be able to overcome his fears by himself.

Contract For Reducing Your Fears

I, _____ commit myself to enter the program for reducing my fear reactions. I will participate fully, in the *Fear Reduction Program.* I will practice the exercises each and every day. Once I have learned the skills of the fear reduction program, I will continue to use them throughout my daily activities. If I should become discouraged, this will not affect me and I will continue working with the program.

A behavioral contract is signed whether the patient is going to work directly with me in therapy or will participate in a fear reduction program on his own.

After you have signed the behavioral contract, the therapy process itself begins. The fear reduction program is divided into the following parts: phobia identification and intensity rating (Chapter 4), relaxation and autogenic training (Chapter 5), and developing the hierarchy and applying it to the desensitization process (Chapter 6).

PART ONE: RELAXATION-AUTOGENIC PROCEDURES

All segments of the fear reduction program are extremely important. No one part will be effective without the entire program.

The training program is designed to be completed within a three week period. A minimum of three daily practice sessions are required. The individual practice session will last from ten to twenty minutes each time.

Part One of the fear reduction program takes one week and involves learning to develop deep relaxation. It may be accomplished in three different ways. These methods can be intermingled, but for best results you should pick one of the formats and follow it through the three weeks.

METHOD A

You will read the instructions and repeat each one of the phrases to yourself, silently. Using this method doesn't require anyone else to help you. An alternative to this method would be to record each day's session into a portable tape recorder and listen to the recording for the specified period of time. This will allow you to attain a better level of passive relaxation and passive concentration.

A housewife who was undergoing the fear reduction program found it extremely convenient to use her son's cassette tape recorder to record all the sessions. Each morning she would take out the required tape and begin the day's practice sessions quickly and easily. This procedure was instrumental in her obtaining maximal results during a seven-day period.

METHOD B

This method may be the most practical for individuals who are hospitalized, convalescent or confined to bed or house. The technique requires that a spouse, or someone who will see the patient on a daily basis for three weeks, participate in the therapy process. The "helper" reads from the practice transcripts provided in this chapter.

Important Note:

Whether you or someone else is recording the practice session into a tape recorder, or a "helper" is verbally providing the training, several rules should be adhered to.

1. You should speak slowly, carefully enunciating each of the words.
2. Words or phrases which require an extra stress are underlined for your convenience.
3. Do not rush. Take your time.
4. Try to develop a rhythmical-flowing texture to your speech.
5. Your voice should not be held abnormally low, but maintain a good quality of resonance.

Remember, you are trying to instill passive relaxation. You are not running a race!

METHOD C

The last and probably most effective method for practicing the procedure, is to have a "helper" pre-record all of the practice sessions on several simple cassette tapes. These cassettes are fairly inexpensive and may be obtained readily at most stores.

The cassette players may range in price from twenty dollars to several hundred. It isn't necessary for you to obtain an expensive cassette recorder, as all recordings for these procedures will be voice only; no music is needed. Cassette tapes come in varying lengths of recording time; the ones you should purchase are sixty-minute cassettes. These tapes will allow thirty minutes recording time on each side. The tapes should be recorded in a quiet environment with as few distracting sounds as possible. Pay special attention to the way in which you record the tapes, as noted above.

Before attempting a recording, you should familiarize yourself thoroughly with a transcript. All tapes should be labeled and numbered in proper progression. As stated earlier, it is advisable to pre-record all of the sessions before starting the therapy. This will insure that the voice used on the tape will be consistently the same. Proper results may take some time and effort. The recording should be done over until satisfactory.

Find someone you know — perhaps a relative or a friend. Tell the person what you are attempting to do and let him or her read this portion of the book. The more thoroughly they understand the intent of their task, the better job they will be able to do.

Do Not Settle for a Poorly Recorded Tape.

RELAXATION TAPE NO. 1

Let's settle back very comfortably now. During the entire course of this session, I want you to listen to my voice. Try not to let any other sounds interfere with your concentration. If anything should distract you, gently push it out of your thoughts and resume concentrating on what I am saying. As I talk to you about each specific part of your body, picture that part in your mind. Each one of the phrases which I present to you should be repeated by yourself, silently, mentally. Do not try to force anything to happen. Just let everything happen very naturally and very comfortably. Remember, you are to use passive relaxation.

You should be lying down or sitting in a very comfortable position. Be sure that your legs are not crossed and allow your hands to be resting on your thighs or by your side.

Remember, you are to repeat each phrase I present to you, silently, mentally, to yourself. Do not change or modify any of the phrases; repeat them exactly as I present them.

> Comfortable position
> Take a deep breath
> Let it out slowly
> Close your eyes
> Repeat each one of the phrases silently to yourself:
> My right arm is heavy
> My right arm is heavy
> My right arm is heavy
> My right arm is heavy
> My right arm is heavy
> My left arm is heavy
> My left arm is heavy
> My left arm is heavy

My left arm is heavy
My left arm is heavy
My arms are heavy
My arms are heavy
My arms are heavy
My arms are heavy
My right leg is heavy
My right leg is heavy
My right leg is heavy
My right leg is heavy
My left leg is heavy
My left leg is heavy
My left leg is heavy
My left leg is heavy
My legs are heavy
My legs are heavy
My legs are heavy
My arms and legs are heavy
My arms and legs are heavy
My arms and legs are heavy
My arms and legs are heavy
My right arm is warm
My right arm is warm
My right arm is warm
My right arm is warm
My right arm is warm
My left arm is warm
My left arm is warm
My left arm is warm
My left arm is warm
My left arm is warm
My arms are warm
My arms are warm
My arms are warm
My right leg is warm
My right leg is warm

My right leg is warm
My right leg is warm
My right leg is warm
My left leg is warm
My left leg is warm
My left leg is warm
My left leg is warm
My left leg is warm
My legs are warm
My legs are warm
My legs are warm
My legs are warm
My legs are warm
My legs are warm
My arms are warm
My arms are warm
My arms are warm
My arms are warm
My arms and legs are warm
My arms and legs are warm
My arms and legs are warm
My arms and legs are warm
My arms and legs are warm
My arms and legs are heavy and warm
My arms and legs are heavy and warm
My arms and legs are heavy and warm
My arms and legs are heavy and warm
My heartbeat is calm and regular
My heartbeat is calm and regular
My heartbeat is calm and regular
My heartbeat is calm and regular
My heartbeat is calm and regular
My heartbeat is calm and regular
My breathing is calm and regular
My breathing is calm and regular
My breathing is calm and regular

My breathing is calm and regular
My stomach is warm
My stomach is warm
My stomach is warm
My stomach is warm
My stomach is warm
My stomach is warm
My forehead is cool
My forehead is cool
My forehead is cool
My forehead is cool
My forehead is cool
I am calm and relaxed
I am calm and relaxed
I am calm and relaxed
I am calm and relaxed
I am calm and relaxed
I am calm and relaxed
The muscles in my arms and legs are loose, limp
and slack
The muscles in my arms and legs are loose, limp
and slack
The muscles in my arms and legs are loose, limp
and slack
The muscles in my arms and legs are loose, limp
and slack
Time to terminate this exercise
Flex your arms
Flex your legs
Take a deep breath
Open your eyes
Get up nice and slowly

RELAXATION TAPE NO. 2
Comfortable position
Take a deep breath

Let it out slowly
Close your eyes
Repeat each one of the phrases silently to yourself
    after I present them
My arms and legs are heavy and warm
My arms and legs are heavy and warm
My arms and legs are heavy and warm
My arms and legs are heavy and warm
My arms and legs are heavy and warm
My heartbeat is calm and regular
My heartbeat is calm and regular
My heartbeat is calm and regular
My heartbeat is calm and regular
My breathing is calm and regular
My breathing is calm and regular
My breathing is calm and regular
My breathing is calm and regular
My stomach is warm
My stomach is warm
My stomach is warm
My stomach is warm
My forehead is cool
My forehead is cool
My forehead is cool
My forehead is cool
My forehead is cool
I feel very calm and quiet
I feel very comfortable and quiet
I am beginning to feel extremely relaxed
I am beginning to feel extremely relaxed
The muscles in my feet feel loose, limp and slack
The muscles in my feet feel loose, limp and slack
My feet feel heavy and relaxed
My feet feel heavy and relaxed
The muscles in my ankles feel loose, limp and slack
The muscles in my ankles feel loose, limp and slack

My ankles feel heavy and relaxed
My ankles feel heavy and relaxed
My knees feel heavy and relaxed
The muscles in my knees feel loose, limp and slack
The muscles in my knees feel loose, limp and slack
My knees feel heavy and relaxed
My knees feel heavy and relaxed
The muscles in my hips are loose, limp and slack
The muscles in my hips are loose, limp and slack
My hips feel heavy and relaxed
My hips feel heavy and relaxed
My hips feel heavy and relaxed
The muscles in my feet, my ankles, my knees and
    my hips are loose, limp and slack
The muscles in my feet, my ankles, my knees and
    my hips are loose, limp and slack
My feet, my ankles, my knees and my hips all feel
    heavy and relaxed
My feet, my ankles, my knees and my hips all feel
    heavy and relaxed
The muscles in my stomach and the whole center
    portion of my body are loose, limp and slack
The muscles in my stomach and the whole center
    portion of my body are loose, limp and slack
My stomach and the whole center portion of my
    body feels heavy and relaxed
My stomach and the whole center portion of my
    body feels heavy and relaxed
The muscles in my hands are loose, limp and slack
The muscles in my hands are loose, limp and slack
My hands feel heavy and relaxed
My hands feel heavy and relaxed
The muscles in my arms are loose, limp and slack
The muscles in my arms are loose, limp and slack
My arms feel heavy and relaxed
My arms feel heavy and relaxed

The muscles in my shoulders are loose, limp and
    slack
The muscles in my shoulders are loose, limp and
    slack
My shoulders feel heavy and relaxed
My shoulders feel heavy and relaxed
The muscles in my hands, my arms, and my shoulders
    are all loose, limp and slack
The muscles in my hands, my arms, and my shoulders
    are all loose, limp and slack
My hands, my arms and my shoulders all feel
    heavy and relaxed
My hands, my arms and my shoulders all feel
    heavy and relaxed
The muscles in my neck are loose, limp and slack
The muscles in my neck are loose, limp and slack
My neck feels heavy and relaxed
My neck feels heavy and relaxed
The muscles in my jaw are heavy and relaxed
The muscles in my jaw are loose, limp and slack
The muscles in my jaw are loose, limp and slack
My jaw feels heavy and relaxed
My jaw feels heavy and relaxed
The muscles in my forehead feel loose, limp and
    slack
The muscles in my forehead are loose, limp and
    slack
My forehead feels heavy and relaxed
My forehead feels heavy and relaxed
The muscles in my neck, my jaw and my forehead
    are all loose, limp and slack
The muscles in my neck, my jaw and my forehead
    are all loose, limp and slack
My neck, my jaw and my forehead all feel heavy
    and relaxed

My neck, my jaw and my forehead all feel heavy
and relaxed
My whole body feels loose, limp and slack
My whole body feels heavy and relaxed
My whole body feels heavy and relaxed
My breathing is getting deeper and deeper
Time to terminate this exercise
Flex your arms
Flex your legs
Take a deep breath
Open your eyes

RELAXATION TAPE NO. 3

Comfortable position
Take a deep breath
Let it out slowly
Close your eyes
My arms and legs are heavy and warm
My arms and legs are heavy and warm
My heartbeat is calm and regular
My heartbeat is calm and regular
My breathing is calm and regular
My breathing is calm and regular
My stomach is warm
My stomach is warm
My forehead is cool
My forehead is cool
My arms and legs are heavy and warm
My heartbeat is calm and regular
My breathing is calm and regular
My stomach is warm
My forehead is cool
I am calm and relaxed
The top of my head feels warm and heavy
The top of my head feels warm and heavy
The relaxing warmth flows into my right shoulder

My right shoulder feels warm and heavy
My right shoulder feels warm and heavy
All of the muscles in my right shoulder are loose,
  limp, and slack
All of the muscles in my right shoulder are loose,
  limp, and slack
My breathing is getting deeper and deeper
The relaxing warmth flows down to my right hand
My right hand feels warm and heavy
My right hand feels warm and heavy
All of the muscles in my right hand are loose, limp,
  and slack
The relaxing warmth flows back up to my right
  arm
My right arm feels warm and heavy
My right arm feels warm and heavy
All of the muscles in my right arm are loose, limp,
  and slack
The relaxing warmth spreads up through my right
  elbow into my right shoulder
My right elbow, my right shoulder, feel warm and
  heavy
My right elbow, my right shoulder, feel warm and
  heavy
All of the muscles in my right elbow, my right
  shoulder, are loose, limp, and slack
The relaxing warmth flows slowly throughout my
  whole back
The warmth is relaxing my back
My back feels warm and heavy
My back feels warm and heavy
All of the muscles in my back are loose, limp, and
  slack
The relaxing warmth moves up my back and into
  my neck
My neck feels warm and heavy

My neck feels warm and heavy
All of the muscles in my neck are loose, limp, and
    slack
All of the muscles in my neck are loose, limp and
    slack
The relaxing warmth flows into my left shoulder
My left shoulder feels warm and heavy
My left shoulder feels warm and heavy
All of the muscles in my left shoulder are loose,
    limp, and slack
All of the muscles in my left shoulder are loose,
    limp and slack
My breathing is getting deeper and deeper
The relaxing warmth flows down to my left hand
My left hand feels warm and heavy
All of the muscles in my left hand are loose, limp,
    and slack
All of the muscles in my left hand are loose, limp,
    and slack
The relaxing warmth flows back up to my left arm
My left arm feels warm and heavy
My left arm feels warm and heavy
All of the muscles in my left arm are loose, limp,
    and slack
All of the muscles in my left arm are loose, limp,
    and slack
The relaxing warmth gradually spreads up through
    my left elbow into my left shoulder
My left elbow, my left shoulder, feel warm and
    heavy
My left elbow, my left shoulder, feel warm and
    heavy
All of the muscles in my left elbow, my left shoulder
    are loose, limp, and slack
All of the muscles in my left elbow, my left shoulder,
    are loose, limp, and slack

The relaxing warmth flows to my heart
My heart feels warm and easy
My heart feels warm and easy
My heartbeat is calm and regular
My heartbeat is calm and regular
The relaxing warmth flows down into my stomach
My stomach feels warm
My stomach feels warm
My breathing is deeper and deeper
My breathing is calm and regular
The relaxing warmth flows down into my right
    thigh
My right thigh feels warm and heavy
My right thigh feels warm and heavy
All of the muscles in my right thigh are loose, limp,
    and slack
All of the muscles in my right thigh are loose, limp,
    and slack
The relaxing warmth flows down into my right foot
My right foot feels warm and heavy
My right foot feels warm and heavy
All of the muscles in my right foot are loose, limp,
    and slack
All of the muscles in my right foot are loose, limp,
    and slack
The relaxing warmth flows slowly up through my
    right calf to my right knee to my right thigh
My right leg feels warm and heavy
My right leg feels warm and heavy
All of the muscles in my right leg are loose, limp,
    and slack
All of the muscles in my right leg are loose, limp,
    and slack
My breathing is deeper and deeper
My breathing is deeper and deeper
The relaxing warmth flows down into my left thigh

My left thigh feels warm and heavy
My left thigh feels warm and heavy
All of the muscles in my left thigh are loose, limp,
  and slack
All of the muscles in my left thigh are loose, limp,
  and slack
The relaxing warmth flows down into my left foot
My left foot feels warm and heavy
My left foot feels warm and heavy
All of the muscles in my left foot are loose, limp,
  and slack
All of the muscles in my left foot are loose, limp,
  and slack
The relaxing warmth flows slowly up through my
  left calf to my left knee to my left thigh
My left leg feels warm and heavy
My left leg feels warm and heavy
All of the muscles in my left leg are loose, limp,
  and slack
All of the muscles in my left leg are loose, limp,
  and slack
My breathing is deeper and deeper
My breathing is deeper and deeper
The relaxing warmth moves up through my stomach
  and into my heart
My heart feels warm
My heart feels warm
I am calm and relaxed
I am calm and relaxed
Time to terminate this exercise
Flex your arms
Flex your legs
Take a deep breath
Open your eyes

RELAXATION TAPE NUMBER 4

By the time you reach this session, you should have obtained a fairly adequate comprehension of the autogenic training procedure. When you take a deep breath and let it out slowly, some of the autogenic responses will begin to occur automatically. At this point I would like to mention that it is imperative that you practice these exercises daily. Remember, you cannot practice too much. You must reach a level at which the autogenic response becomes automatic.

>   Comfortable position
>   Take a deep breath
>   Let it out slowly
>   Close your eyes
>   My arms and legs are heavy and warm
>   My arms and legs are heavy and warm
>   My arms and legs are heavy and warm
>   My arms and legs are heavy and warm
>   My arms and legs are heavy and warm
>   My heartbeat is calm and regular
>   My heartbeat is calm and regular
>   My heartbeat is calm and regular
>   My heartbeat is calm and regular
>   My heartbeat is calm and regular
>   My heartbeat is calm and regular
>   My heartbeat is calm and regular
>   My breathing is calm and regular
>   My breathing is calm and regular
>   My stomach is warm
>   My stomach is warm
>   My stomach is warm
>   My stomach is warm
>   My stomach is warm
>   My forehead is cool
>   My forehead is cool

My forehead is cool
My forehead is cool
My forehead is cool
I am calm and relaxed
I am calm and relaxed
My brain works automatically
My brain works automatically
My brain works automatically
My anxiety is getting less each day
My anxiety is getting less each day
My anxiety is getting less each day
My anxiety is getting less each day
Fears no longer bother me
Fears no longer bother me
Fears no longer bother me
I can relax at any time
I can rclax at any time
I can relax at any time
Fears no longer bother me
I can relax at any time
Fears no longer bother me
I can get rid of any phobias I want
I can get rid of any phobias I want
I can get rid of any phobias I want
I can get rid of any phobias I want
I am calm and relaxed
I am calm and relaxed
I am calm and relaxed
Fears and phobias no longer bother me
Fears and phobias no longer bother me
Fears and phobias no longer bother me
Fears and phobias no longer bother me
[Substitute ____ no longer causes anxiety for me
your specific__no longer causes anxiety for me
phobia]_____no longer causes anxiety for me
_____no longer causes anxiety for me

——————no longer causes anxiety for me
Time to terminate this exercise
Flex your arms
Flex your legs
Take a deep breath
Open your eyes

RELAXATION TAPE NUMBER 5

I am calm and relaxed
Anxiety flows from my body
Anxiety flows from my body
Anxiety flows from my body
Anxiety flows from my body
I am calm and relaxed
I am calm and relaxed
Tension flows from my body
Tension flows from my body
Tension flows from my body
Tension flows from my body
Anxiety and tension flow from my body
Anxiety and tension flow from my body
Anxiety and tension flow from my body
Anxiety and tension flow from my body
I am becoming phobia free
I am becoming phobia free
I am becoming phobia free
I am becoming phobia free
I can stop thinking my fears
I can stop thinking my fears
I can stop thinking my fears
I can stop thinking my fears
My life is relaxed
My life is relaxed
My life is relaxed
My life is relaxed
I check my body for tension

I check my body for tension
I am phobia free and flying high
I am phobia free and flying high
I am phobia free and flying high
I am phobia free and flying high
My body functions better without fear and anxiety
My body functions better without fear and anxiety
My body functions better without fear and anxiety
Time to terminate this exercise
Flex your arms
Flex your legs
Take a deep breath
Open your eyes

NOTE: From this point onward, you may practice each one of these sessions in its entirety or take selected portions of an exercise and develop a routine which works the best for you. Be sure to use only the sentences which I have provided but you may change their order of combination.

SCHEDULE FOR PART 1 OF THE FEAR REDUCTION PROGRAM

Day 1 — Use relaxation session number 1 a minimum of three times. [If you encounter problems, go back and review the required posture and technique. Chapter 5]

Day 2 — Use relaxation session number 1 at least three times during this day. [Although you will be moving on to relaxation session number 2, shortly, there will always be positive benefits derived from going back and reviewing session number 1 occasionally]

Day 3 — Use relaxation session number 2 at least three times during the day. [Devote the end of one of the sessions to a review of the relaxation procedures used in session number 1]

Day 4 — Use relaxation session number 2 at least three times during the day.

Day 5 — Use relaxation session number 3 at least three times during the day. [Use the end of one session for a review of session 2]

Day 6 — Use relaxation session 4 at least three times during this day. [Review session number 2 and 3]

Note: The review session may be used as an extra [fourth] session for a day.

Day 7 — This will be the final day of your programmed relaxation training. This in no way means that you will stop using this method. Relaxation session number 5 is to be practiced on the seventh day a minimum of three times. From that point on, relaxation session number 5 will be practiced a minimum of three times daily for at least 15 minutes each time. Session number 5 will be continued for the remaining two weeks of the program. If during those three weeks, you decide to go back and review any one of the previous sessions, please feel free to do so.

Remember, you are to fill in the daily report form upon completing each session. This record is to be kept for the entire three weeks of the program.

Daily Relaxation Report Form

Set up your program for a minimum of three practice sessions each day. Record the date and time of the session. Determine your Pre-Session level of tension by deciding on a number from 1 to 20, with 1 being the most relaxed you could possibly be and 20 representing maximum tension. Go through the program exercises, then record the Post-Session value on a scale of 1 to 20.

SIGNS OF SELF RELAXATION

1. A feeling of heaviness in the arms or legs. This heaviness may be felt in all limbs at the same time or one arm and one leg.
2. Breathing is slow and regular. There is no feeling that you need to gasp for breath. The breathing pattern is very rhythmical and deep.
3. The heartbeat is regular and steady. There are no fluctuating increases or decreases in the heart rate.
4. There is a slight tingling sensation in the hands or feet.

5. There is a feeling of drowsiness or sleepiness.
6. Your jaw feels heavy.
7. Your shoulders are drooping slightly; they are not held in an up-tight rigid position.
8. Sounds seem to become distant.

You may not experience these sensations in the exact way I have described them. The way each individual experiences the body sensations of relaxation will differ. Use the above list to serve as a constant check of your ability to relax.

Date	Pre-Session Tension	Post-Session Tension	Note any areas of your body where you still feel tension

Date	Pre-Session Tension	Post-Session Tension	Note any areas of your body where you still feel tension

WHEN DO I PRACTICE?

Experience shows that it is better to practice at specified times during the day and to repeat your sessions at these times on a daily basis than to practice randomly. Until your training period is over and you have acquired sufficient expertise in using the relaxation-autogenics, practice should consist of a session in the morning immediately after awakening, a session towards mid-day, and a final session approximately one hour before you go to sleep. It is extremely important that you practice at the same time each day. You are attempting to develop a habit and in order to establish this habit firmly in your daily routine you must maintain the same practice times each day.

The practice times for the weekend should also be the same as on week days.

No excuses! Set up your practice times and stick with them.

CAN I PRACTICE MORE THAN THREE TIMES A DAY?

An inherent advantage of this system is that you can never overdose through practicing too much. Do not neglect your daily activities at home or work for the sake of practicing an extra time or two. The program plan calls for three [15 min.] sessions a day. If you think you'll never find enough time to practice, stop and think how much time you actually waste during the course of one day. Multiply that by seven days and you will be surprised to discover how much time is wasted during one week.

WILL MY PRACTICE SESSIONS ALWAYS BE 15 MINUTES?

In the beginning, it is essential that you maintain the 15 minute practice sessions, three times daily. Once you have obtained proficiency in the relaxation-autogenic method, then you will be able to achieve the state of relaxation in a shorter period of time. Do not rush this for the entire method needs to become firmly ingrained into your behavior patterns. After practicing for several weeks, you will definitely notice that you require less time to obtain a deep state of relaxation, and you will then be able to reduce the length of your practice sessions slightly.

If you follow the training charts, there will be a time when your scores will indicate that the three standard practice sessions a day may be reduced to two sessions and the time shortened. Do not guess when this should occur. Use the report forms and let them serve as your guide.

WILL I HAVE TO KEEP THE SAME POSITIONS DURING ALL THE PRACTICE SESSIONS?

The answer to this question is no. When you become proficient at the relaxation-autogenics, you should begin to vary your relaxation positions. It would be very nice if all of us were able to immediately find a very comfortable chair to relax into whenever a stressful or fear-producing situation presented itself. Unfortunately, life is not that easy. It is important therefore when you reach level four on the programmed relaxation scale, to begin varying your positions. Varying a position should first be tried by changing seats. If you have been lying down during these exercises, then you should try sitting in a chair.

Do not flit from one position to the next. If you have been reclining during your training sessions and wish to try the relaxation-autogenics in a more upright position, then stick to this new position until you are able to obtain the desired results. As with anything new, you must give it a chance. Just because you are able to maintain a good sense of relaxation while reclining does not automatically mean that you'll immediately be able to transfer what you have learned to a more erect position.

Gradually, you should try several different positions and eventually you will be able to perform the procedure while standing and walking.

Quite obviously, if you are standing and walking around your eyes cannot be closed. This is one of the most crucial steps in the entire relaxation process and should be approached with great patience. Most people take many sessions to achieve the relaxation-autogenic state with their eyes open. If you are ever to use this process during real-life fear-producing situations, it is essential that you be able to achieve at least a mild sense of relaxation while keeping your eyes open.

After gaining proficiency with the eyes open, you will be able to use specific portions of this therapy while walking, attending meetings, watching television or progressing through your normal daily activities. To quote a patient who had developed the ability to use relaxation autogenic methods with his eyes open while at work: "It's super. I never realized how uptight I was during the day. Now, nothing bothers me and the more I practice, the easier it gets. I think I'm going to do this for the rest of my life."

WHAT ABOUT MY DOCTOR?

"Does this mean I may never have to see a doctor again?" Of course not. Anytime you notice physical symptoms which might relate to some disease process, you should immediately consult your physician. However, with increasing relaxation, there is a definite possibility that you may experience fewer colds, less sick time from work and an overall increase in your level of activity with less fatigue.

THE WHO, WHAT, WHERE AND HOW OF YOUR PHOBIA

After deciding which phobia you are going to work on first,

and before you begin constructing a hierarchy for getting rid of that phobia, we need to define exactly what is involved in the specific phobic situation. Before going any further, be sure that you have completed the form below which will help you in constructing a better hierarchy. Fill in all the spaces completely. Do not rush this test, take your time and make sure that you have answered the who, what, where, and how aspects of the phobia. Now take a plain sheet of paper and copy down the questions on the left hand side of the blank sheet, making sure to leave plenty of space between questions so that you can fill in the important information. After completing the form, use it in constructing the hierarchy.

Who is involved?: _____
What are the cir-
cumstances?: _____
Where does it take
place?: _____
How would you like
to behave?: _____

PART TWO: CONSTRUCTING THE HIERARCHY
After identifying your phobias and calculating their intensity, you must practice the relaxation methods diligently. While you are going through the relaxation-autogenic process, Part Two, construction of the hierarchy, can be initiated.

There are three basic ways to construct a hierarchy and all three will be explained below.

1. As an example, let's say your phobic reaction is towards flying in airplanes. First, sit down in a nice quiet place and have before you a stack of 3×5 cards. It will be good to have approximately 20-25 cards, in case you make any mistakes and have to redo a card. You will be filling out 15 cards and each card will contain a brief descriptive sentence or two. These descriptions should be kept as short as possible. You are to label the first card #1 and begin with the least anxiety-producing scene that you can

think of involving an airplane flight. As an example, this might be the sentence; "Jim has just mentioned to me that we are going to fly to California on vacation." This is a simple statement of intent to go on an airplane flight. The card could serve as #1 with the remaining cards describing preparations for the flight, eventual drive to the airport, inside the airport, boarding the airplane and finally take-off and flight-landing.

After completing the fifteen cards, set them aside and let them sit for a day or two while you are working on your relaxation exercises.

SETTING THE "SUDS" SCALE

The "Subjective Units of Disturbance Scale" (Wolpe and Lazarus, 1966: Wolpe, 1973) will be used to help you put the scenes in the right order. As I have said before, the scenes need to be arranged from the one which produces only slight anxiety to the card which causes the most fear.

The intensity of anxiety induced by scenes on the cards should increase in a gradual manner so that the transition from one card to the next will be a smooth one. By assigning each card a numerical rating in the upper right hand corner, you form a "SUDS" scale. A rating of 0 represents a state of total relaxation or non-fear. The highest rating is 100 for the most frightening and anxiety-producing aspect of your phobia.

Now designate a SUDS on the right hand corner of each one of the cards you have written out before proceeding with desensitization. Do not assign the same number to more than one card.

In no case should there be a gap of more than 20 points between cards as this may cause a poor transition from one card to the next. If this happens, you will have to insert an intermediate card.

Take the cards up again and sort through them, making sure they are in order of increasing intensity. At this time you may want to revise several of the cards to make them more concise or graphic.

A new set of cards will be made for each one of the phobias. If you find a need for more than fifteen cards, then you should go back and make your statements more concise. Too many cards will prolong the desensitization process. Examples of hierarchies have been given in Chapter 6. Please feel free to use them in their exact form or modify them for your own usage. The scenes on the card should be graphic enough so that you can readily visualize and obtain a fear response from simply reading them.

2. The second method of constructing the hierarchy would be to take the fifteen hierarchy cards which you have developed in Step #1 and sorting through magazines or periodicals, cut out pictures which might lend themselves to the descriptive statements on the cards. If your card states; ''The plane is beginning to take off and the nose wheel is lifting off the ground,'' then you might cut out a picture of an airplane taking off from the runway. Go through each one of the cards and find a picture suitable for the description. If you find it impossible to get a picture for every card, then get a picture for as many as possible. These pictures are then to be taped or glued on a sheet of paper and placed behind each of the appropriate cards. When you next read the card about taking off from the airport, you will flip the card and immediately see the picture and then, closing your eyes, you will be able to obtain a better visual image. As with the cards, there should be no more than fifteen pictures in a set.

One of the advantages to this technique is that you can pick the picture and scenes which have definite fear-evoking properties for you in particular. Remember, do not be too easy on yourself. It is important that you develop the hierarchy from the least fear-producing card and then work upwards.

3. The third method involves a combined usage of the pictures, hierarchy cards and cassette recorder. If your hierarchy is for the fear of airplanes, use the hierarchy cards which were developed in phase No. 1. Insert the pictures behind each one of the appropriate cards. The cards should now be in the proper order from the least anxiety-provoking to the most fear-producing.

After these two steps have been completed, take the cassette tape recorder and record the exact phrases on each one of the cards. You should allow a five-minute gap between each one of the phrases.

The sequence will proceed as follows: (1) You will read the first card and look at the appropriate picture. Close your eyes and turn on the tape recorder. (2) As you listen to the tape, visualize the picture you have just seen. Using your imagination, try to gain the full impact of the tape recording and visualization of the picture.

Once the hierarchy has been completed, it is then time to move on to the desensitization process.

PART 3: DESENSITIZATION

We are about to embark on the final step of the fear reduction program. Desensitization has been explained to you in Chapter 6 and if you have any questions regarding this technique, a quick review of the chapter would be in order.

Before attempting this final step, you should be able to obtain at least four of the body responses during 80 percent of your relaxation training exercises. Do not try to rush ahead. People who try this last step without adequately mastering the relaxation skills, only heighten the chances of failure.

As we have said in Chapter 6, we are attempting to pair a normally fear-producing stimulus with a relaxation response.

We have presented you with several methods for constructing the hierarchy and different methods for its presentation. Find the method which is most comfortable for you to use. In all cases we will be starting with the least anxiety-provoking situation. In other words, card number 1 will be the first of the sequence.

The exact steps of the process are outlined below.

1. Assume your relaxation position, and spend a few minutes allowing your body to lose its tension.
2. Look at the first card (or have it presented on audio tape) and visualize that scene as vividly and clearly as possible. It is always best to try to imagine yourself in that actual

scene. Take at least thirty seconds to let the visualization have its fullest impact.

3. Activate your autogenic response through silent repetition of the autogenic phrases (this can also be done through the tape recorder, but is found to be most effective if it can be accomplished by the subject, through silent repetition.)

4. While you are visualizing the scene, continue to use your autogenics.

5. When you can visualize the scene and experience at least four of the body responses of relaxation (p. 149) then this is your indicator to move onto the next card.

NOTE: If you find yourself working on one particular card for more than two days, then you have moved too fast and should regress back to a card where you can obtain the four needed body responses. Stay with this successful card for at least one day and try progressing more slowly through the hierarchy. Usually by reducing the quickness of your pace, success on the difficult hierarchies can be assured.

Use the daily report form, to record your progress through the hierarchy. This will serve as an invaluable tool in determining your progress.

Card #	Date	Number of Body Responses	Card #	Date	Number of Body Responses

Card #	Date	Number of Body Responses	Card #	Date	Number of Body Responses

QUESTIONS AND ANSWERS

HOW DO I KNOW WHEN I'M READY TO TRY THE HIER-ARCHY?

When you are achieving at least four of the signs of self-relaxation, then you are ready to proceed with the first step of the anxiety hierarchy. Do not start this hierarchy if you have obtained only two or three of the required responses, even if it is the third week. Do not start the third week until you have the correct amount of relaxation. Many people are misled and after experiencing only three of the required responses, go to the hierarchy. They may not experience any problem with the elementary steps of the hierarchy, but as it proceeds, they will definitely lose much of the effectiveness in the program.

CAN I USE THE REQUIRED BODY SENSATIONS AS A CHECK TO SEE HOW I AM DOING?

Yes, At anytime during your program, you can check yourself to see that you are gaining the required body responses, Remember, you are not to go to the next higher step until you have gained four body responses while participating in that hierarchy step.

HOW MANY TIMES WILL I HAVE TO EXPERIENCE ONE STEP ON THE HIERARCHY?

No one can tell you how many attempts you will require to pass on to the next step in the hierarchy. The best way to gauge your progress is through using the body response method. This will serve as an indicator of your progress.

SHOULD I WORK ON THIS FOR MANY HOURS DURING THE DAY?

No. Work on the hierarchy can be overdone and therefore should be limited to no more than one and half hours per day. As with any other type of activity, you will become fatigued and your level of performance will diminish.

CHAPTER EIGHT
Alternate Methods

*"He who strikes terror into others is
himself in continual fear."*

CLAUDIAN

In addition to autogenics and desensitization, several other
methods are useful in helping you overcome phobias. They can
be used alone or together with the methods already described.

These additional therapies will be divided into two distinct
classes: self-help therapies you can learn and use by yourself, and
therapies which would require you to see a therapist.

In the first section of self-help therapies, each method will be
described, with appropriate case studies, so that you can understand how the process works. Exercises will also be included to
help you learn the method.

PART ONE: HELP YOURSELF

The phobia reduction methods I am including at this point in the
book should not be treated as "second-class citizens" in the
world of fear treatment, but as another way of conquering your
anxiety. Whether your anxiety is current and ongoing or anticipatory (the fear generated by thoughts of things which might
happen in the future), the following techniques may be extremely
helpful in reducing your phobias.

PHOBIA REHEARSAL

Phobia rehearsal is a method you can practice at anytime during the day to help reduce your fears. Its purpose is to give you the positive experience of overcoming your fears.

By mentally picturing yourself successfully overcoming fear, you start the programming process in your brain to extinguish the fear reaction. An example of this would be a man who is fearful of taking tests. Every time his driver's license comes up for renewal, he scores very poorly on the written part of the test, in spite of knowing the answers to the questions. Using phobia rehearsal, he would mentally rehearse the phobia reduction by visualizing the whole process of walking into the room, sitting down to take the test, taking the test, and receiving a passing grade from the examiner. He could embellish the scene as much as he likes as long as he continues to visualize a positive outcome.

Similar to this is a method developed by Dr. Alan Kazdin, an associate professor of psychology at Penn State University, which he calls success rehearsal. In this technique, you recreate scenes which cause fear in your mind, and then imagine someone else successfully coping with the anxiety situation. This gives you a model or example of how the situation should be handled and you can then follow through on your own and overcome the fear.

I personally know many people who have used this type of positive mental exercise to learn how to fly successfully, pass their bar examination, overcome text anxiety, or fear of animals and phobic situations involving meeting or working with other people.

Richard Suinn (1976) has developed a novel method of applying behavioral rehearsal, which he calls visuo-motor behavioral rehearsal, or VMBR. He is best known for his use of this method to teach competitive skiing. Ski racers can mentally practice racing techniques and actually win races on the basis of their mental preparation. A college team won its league championship after working with Suinn, and numerous skiers have experienced improvement in their performance. The United States Nordic

Cross-Country Relay Team was involved in behavioral rehearsal and improved its performance level. I recently used phobia rehearsal with a group of gymnasts who were able to reduce their level of anxiety and significantly improve their performance in competition.

Remember, it is important that you visualize your success clearly and that you follow through the phobia rehearsal to a positive and successful conclusion. At first this may take some practice, but as soon as you are able to enter that elevator mentally or walk along a dark street mentally, then you will find it much easier to develop more detailed mental images and eventually adapt the mental images to a real life situation. The more detail you can include in your phobia rehearsal, the more impact it will have on reducing your fear when you actually encounter the situation in real life.

RULES FOR PHOBIA REHEARSAL
1. The imagined scenes must be something you plan to encounter or do in the near future. Do not rehearse something that may or may not happen five years from now. Make the scene important to you right now.
2. You are going to imagine a model who will help you through the fearful situation. By imitating the model's behavior, through mental imagery, you will experience coping with your fears and carrying through the fearful scene.
3. The model may be someone you know or even a celebrity. Pick a model of the same sex and approximately your age. Select a model you KNOW WILL BE ABLE TO COMPLETE THE TASK SUCCESS-FULLY.
4. The scene must always come to a positive conclusion (overcoming the fear). Model selection is therefore extremely important.

Step 1 — Take a piece of paper. Briefly describe the fearful situation. If you have already done this with the hierarchy cards, then you may use these instead of a scene description. The hierarchy cards will have to be modified to include the following three essential ingredients:

1. The model *confronts the fearful situation.*
2. The model *expresses his or her fear reaction, but immediately begins the relaxation exercises.*
3. The model is *reinforced for successfully completing the scene.*

Step 2 — Allow yourself to get into the most comfortable position possible. Obtain a good state of relaxation and starting with the first scene, begin your imaginary movie. In this movie, you and your model will confront the fearful situation. Both you and the model will experience the fear reaction but the model will resolve the fearful reaction through relaxation. You are to imagine yourself relaxing and following the model's example. The movie will continue with you and the model completing the task whether it be petting a dog, riding in an airplane, or giving a speech in front of a large audience.

Step 3 — The running of your mental movie should take no longer than 10 minutes and should be repeated at least twice a day for two weeks. After running the movie several times, you may find it necessary to revise some of your scene cards.

REMEMBER: ALL PHOBIA REHEARSAL MOVIES END SUCCESSFULLY!

Step 4 — Now it is time for you to place yourself within the fearful situation in real life. This should only be attempted after you feel comfortable with the phobia rehearsal method. When experiencing the phobia in real life, try to imitate exactly the way in which the model reacts. If necessary, keep visualizing the movie while you are actually going through the situation.

Step 5 — Repeat the mental movie and practice real life situations until you notice a definite decrease in your fear reaction. At this point, the mental movies may be reduced.

NOW IT IS TIME TO RIDE THE ELEVATOR, TAKE AN
AIRPLANE TRIP, OR ANYTHING ELSE YOU MIGHT
FEAR.

Arthur B. had been employed by a large company for ten
years. He was a hard worker and well respected by fellow
employees. However, he had been upset for several months, ever
since a junior employee was promoted over him into a superv-
isory position. Arthur felt that his work record and seniority
should have gained him the new position. He wanted to confront
his boss about the problem, but was afraid of repercussions. Even
thinking about talking to his boss about the situation brought
butterflies to his stomach and he would start to stammer.

First, I had Arthur pick a movie star who was approximately
his age and who he felt could be assertive in this type of situation.
Next, I had Arthur create a movie with the scene cards in which
he and the model went up to the boss and confronted him about
the promotion.

The scenes went as follows:
1. Arthur and the model decide to confront the boss about the
   promotion. Arthur is impressed by the model's determina-
   tion and assertive behavior.
2. While sitting in the boss's waiting room, Arthur's movie
   shows the model becoming nervous along with Arthur. The
   model uses the relaxation exercises to become calm and
   therefore block the fear reaction.
3. They continue with the relaxation techniques as Arthur and
   the model confront the boss and discuss the problem.
4. During the discussion with the boss, the model stammers at
   times and appears to be blocking his relaxation responses.
   But by continuing to try to relax, the model is able to
   overcome his nervousness and the movie ends with Arthur
   receiving a satisfactory response from his boss.

Arthur practiced this for three weeks, at least twice a day. By the time he was ready to enact the scene in real life, he was extremely confident of his ability to be assertive in front of his boss.

His last comment to me was very encouraging. "I know that I can do it now and even if I don't get the promotion, I'll feel better about myself for confronting the situation."

In actuality Arthur did not get a promotion at that time; but within two months, when the next position was made available, Arthur was offered the advancement.

OBSESSIVE-COMPULSIVE BEHAVIORS

When a person's fear and anxiety become unbearable, he may develop an obsessive-compulsive reaction. The trademark of the obsessive-compulsive is that he or she becomes totally preoccupied with recurring thoughts and actions which cannot be extinguished. An individual's obsessive-compulsive behavior may be very unpleasant and painful, such as an urge to hit a boss, or rather harmless, such as avoiding touching anything the color of red.

Obsessive-compulsive patients whom I've worked with appear to be overcome with worry and self-doubt. They have a tremendous fear that they have failed to do something which will insure their own welfare and possibly the welfare of their family or loved ones. I once had a patient who was so worried that he was forgetting to do something that his obsessive-compulsive double-checking took most of his time and therefore he was never able to accomplish very much. People such as this patient are extremely threatened whenever they are forced to make a decision about the future.

To help you better understand what obsessive-compulsive people are like, take the following examples of two fictional characters. Captain Queeg, in the *The Caine Mutiny,* was obsessed with order. Whenever his routine or the ship's routine was disrupted, this threw him into an absolute panic. As you may remember, his men took advantage of this and drove him into deeper obsession. The continued ritual of rubbing ball bearings

in his hand was the compulsive aspect of hi
example can be found in Captain Ahab, the ca
Moby Dick. Captain Ahab became obsessed with his desi
the white whale, which had taken off his leg. Because of his
obsession to kill the whale, all his acts became compulsively
directed towards that end.

I am sure that you know obsessive-compulsive people. Some
of these people may not be as severely affected as the ones
mentioned, but the obsessive-compulsive behavior does limit
their ability to enjoy life and in most cases, these people are
extremely unproductive. So much time and energy is spent maintaining their obsessive-compulsive behavior that very little else is
accomplished.

Take a few moments now to examine some of your behaviors
and see if you are acting in an obsessive or compulsive manner.

Do you repeat acts over and over again?

Are certain thoughts constantly in your head which you cannot
get out?

Are you constantly worried about the future?

Does it seem like you're always planning and never getting
anything done?

If you can answer yes to any of the above questions, then
there's a possibility that you have some degree of obsessive or
compulsive behavior. There is also a chance you may have a
combination of the two behaviors. Even in its minor forms,
obsessive-compulsive behavior can be unpleasant for you and
confusing to those around you.

A woman who has a phobic reaction towards spiders may
become obsessive in her thinking about the object of her fear. The
harder she tries not to think about spiders, the more they come
into mind. She very soon begins looking around corners, under
furniture, and behind doors to make sure that no spiders are
present. Avoiding any contact with spiders becomes an obsession
and may eventually direct a good portion of her activities and
actually increase the likelihood of her encountering a spider.

Compulsions may also be understood as an attempt by an

individual to overcome his phobic and fear reactions. Compulsions usually involve rather aimless but constantly repetitive acts such as counting, talking to one's self or touching objects. These compulsive behaviors may develop from a phobic reaction and any attempt to stop the behavior without the proper technique will invariably increase the individual's anxiety level.

THOUGHT STOPPING

The harder the patient tries to force the obsessive thought out of his mind, the more frequently it returns. In order to stop such thoughts a special procedure must be conducted called thought-stopping.

The therapist will ask the patient to verbalize the fear-evoking situation and in the middle of the explanation, the therapist will shout, "Stop!" This is repeated several times in an attempt to actually stop the thought process. The patient is then taught to use this procedure himself. Whenever he finds his thoughts turning towards the fear-producing situation, he will give himself a non-verbal message to stop! Thought-stopping has proven to be an excellent device in some of the fear evoking situations that have reached an obsessional level. The ability to shout "Stop," mentally has been found to have great value in the treatment of true obsessional behavior related to phobias.

Repetitive, negativistic, fear producing thoughts can also be stopped without the help of a therapist. Whenever you find yourself "THINKING FEAR," simply say to yourself "STOP!" At first you will shout the word "STOP!" out loud, then eventually you will make the word "STOP!" a mental command.

Dr. David C. Rimm of Old Dominion University has carried the process of thought stopping one step further. After the word "STOP," Dr. Rimm has the patient make an assertive statement. If the person thinks: "I'm going to fail the test," he should say to himself, "STOP!" and then follow that with the statement, "If I study, I know I can do well on the test."

STEP 1: Write down several fearful thoughts you think about repeatedly.

STEP 2: Next to the fearful thought draw an arrow to the right. Then write the word "stop" in bold letters.

STEP 3: Next to the word stop place an arrow and follow it with a positive statement to negate the fearful thought.

FEARFUL THOUGHT → STOP → POSITIVE
STATEMENT

Not all of your phobias come from the outside environment. Many phobias are what I call "thinking your fears." Many of these thoughts can serve as a springboard into the vicious cycle of phobias. You may *think* you're "losing control" or even "going crazy." If you are not able to stop "thinking your fear," then you will probably fulfill your prophecy of anxiety.

What are these "thoughts of fear" that seem to plague people? The following case presents an example of such fear.

James M. was a twenty-nine-year-old man, married with three children. He held a position which provided steady employment but earned him only barely enough to give his family the necessities of living with a small amount left over for their yearly vacation. Advancement was slow and there was little chance to change his type of work.

Slowly, he became increasingly anxious and nervous about the family's money situation. These thoughts were usually prefaced by the "what if" syndrome.

"What if I don't get my raise next year?"

"What if one of the kids gets sick and I can't pay the medical bills?"

"What if the washing machine breaks down and I have to spend the extra money to repair it?"

"What if I get laid off the job?"

One or all of these statements could possibly come true in the future. None of us can predict the future, but James' obsessive thinking about financial disaster caused him to develop a phobic response towards money matters. This anticipatory (thinking fear) was causing a disruption in his family life, his job, and his relationship with other people.

James initiated the thought-stopping procedure and within two weeks was able to control his obsessive fear about finances. He followed the thought-stopping procedure with goal-setting to insure some viable alternatives for his financial future.

James is the perfect example of the effect "thinking a fear" can have upon one's lifestyle.

PART TWO: LET OTHERS HELP YOU

Part 2 of this chapter will focus upon alternative therapies which may be used to reduce your phobias, but should be performed under the direction of a trained therapist. These therapies will be presented briefly and are included only to complete your knowledge about the reduction of fear. They should not be attempted on a "do-it-yourself-basis."

MODELING

Pipe-smoking therapists many times find their patients beginning to smoke pipes. In my own practice, I have frequently become aware of a patient who begins to sit, talk, and react in the same way I do. They are modeling or imitating my behavior.

Dr. Albert Bandura of Stanford University has used a technique of modeling to reduce the fear of snakes in his patients. He feels that imitation may be a very strong therapeutic force. He has successfully treated a large number of patients with snake phobic reactions, by asking them to observe a therapist handling the snake. Usually, the modeling procedure involves the use of a peer model, the same age, who does not display a fear reaction when confronted by the object, individual, or situation that produced the fear in the patient. Some people have referred to this type of therapy as "vicarious" or "spectator" therapy. I have found the use of modeling behavior to be very beneficial in helping to "unfreeze" the fearful behavior of a patient.

CASE

Susan had a fear of cats. This fear had been operating since the age of 8 and she totally avoided pictures, speaking of or especially seeing cats. After gaining a rapport with Susan, I proceeded to desensitize her towards talking about cats and seeing pictures of them. The final step involved bringing a cat into the room and having Susan watch me touch the cat. After two sessions, she was able to begin to imitate my behavior.

This example is somewhat simplified, but does provide the basis for much of the learned behavior in our lives. Modeling accounts for a significant way in which we learn phobic reactions and therefore can be used effectively (under the direction of a therapist) to resolve fear.

GROUP THERAPY

Group therapy can be used effectively to help people reduce their phobic reactions. Within the course of my group therapy, I may use systematic desensitization, modeling, hypnosis, and other methods to help patients reduce their phobic reactions. Whenever I treat a number of people together, I try to group them according to their phobias.

Group therapy for phobia reduction is quite complicated and should only be attempted by experienced and well-trained therapists. Facilitating the reduction of phobias in four to eight people at the same time, requires a thorough knowledge and ability to use the various techniques.

Group therapy has been used effectively in reduction of the fear of flying. By using the relaxation-autogenic techniques, combined with desensitization and certain modeling techniques, the results have been quite beneficial. I personally have used group therapy for the fear of flying only in cases of extreme phobic reaction. Usually, most of the people expressing a flying phobia are capable of using the "self-help" techniques which have been previously outlined in this book.

HYPNOSIS

Hypnosis, as a therapy for phobia reduction, has been used since the time of the early kings of England and France. They believed that certain curative powers resulted from the "laying on of hands." Practices passed on by court magicians and sorcerers were also known as "touching for the king's evil." This belief in miraculous healing had its foundations centuries before Christ. The power of suggestion has been recognized throughout recorded history and many of the accounts found in the Bible and ancient literature refer to a heightened state of suggestability as a result of control of mental and physical processes.

During the middle 1700's, Franz Mesmer developed a thesis based on the premise that the planets influence human health. He believed that this was accomplished by a catalyst of a magnetic-type fluid, in which all our bodies were immersed. He began to treat various diseases through the use of magnets, strategically placed over the area of illness. His results were dramatic and surprising to all his professional colleagues.

Hostility towards him from his colleagues began to grow and very soon Mesmer was forced to leave Vienna. He then moved to Paris and set up his clinic for treating all kinds of diseases.

It was later discovered — through descriptions of his methodology — that Mesmer was simply using the power of suggestion. He would suggest to the patient that the disease process would disappear and by allowing the patient to relax, many of the symptoms did mysteriously go into remission.

This was the beginning of hypnotherapy, and for many years afterward this form of treatment alternated between being in and out of fashion.

Sigmund Freud began experimenting with hypnosis but was disappointed and later dropped it in favor of psychoanalysis, because he was unable to induce a sufficiently deep trance state.

During World War I, hypnosis was used widely as a battlefield technique to reduce pain.

The present-day use of hypnosis is widespread and most medical schools devote a small portion of time to a discussion of the use of hypnosis. Psychologists and psychiatrists have used it for many years to reduce the effects of fear reactions. Hypnosis for the reduction of phobias has proved to be fairly productive but the need for extensive treatments has prevented hypnosis from becoming more widespread. Since the procedure is therapist-directed, the patient must depend upon his or her therapist for constant treatment. Although self-hypnosis may be used, it has been found to be less effective than therapist-induced hypnosis.

Hypnosis therefore lies in a double bind. The method has been proven to be effective in many cases, but by the nature of the technique, it is not a treatment procedure which can be used by the vast majority of people without therapist-directed training. In my own practice, hypnosis has proved useful when the fear reaction is extremely severe or when other psychological problems are present.

Hypnosis has been very useful in the treatment of symptoms related to chronic phobic responses (fear, anxiety and physical dysfunctions), but as in the use of medications, it only treats the symptoms and not the cause.

As an example, if I were to use hypnosis for the treatment of insomnia, I would be able to suggest to the subject that sleep would be easily attained and that he would be able to sleep through the entire night and awaken very relaxed and refreshed in the morning. The number of sessions required to produce this effect would depend upon the subject's susceptibility to hypnosis and the intensity of the insomnia. Let's assume that I am able, through the use of hypnosis, to induce six to eight hours sleep for the patient. However, if I were to cease the hypnotic suggestion for sleep, the patient would again revert to insomnia. Therefore, we have masked the cause of the patient's insomnia by treating only the symptom. I would mention at this time that through prolonged sessions of hypnotherapy I would be able to define the cause of this patient's insomnia but as stated before, this would be a long and expensive procedure.

The previous example could be used in cases involving facial tics, nail biting, stuttering, colitis and many other physical and emotional manifestations of anxiety and fear.

In my practice, I have occasionally found it necessary to use hypnosis to enhance the relaxation-autogenic training process. If, after several trials, the patient is still unable to obtain the needed levels of relaxation training, then I may use hypnotic suggestion to speed up the therapy process. The hypnotic suggestion would be in the form that follows:

> "Now that you are deeply asleep — I want you to listen to my voice and you will be able to do everything that I tell you for your own good and well being. At all times, you are in complete control and you will remember everything when you awaken. Day by day, slowly, but surely, you will find that relaxation will be easier for you to obtain. You will no longer try too hard. The next time you try the relaxation-autogenic training you will be able to give yourself up completely to these very relaxed and wonderful feelings. Each time you try the method your relaxation and control will become deeper."

Hypnosis can be a useful adjunct to the complete phobia reduction process. Hypnosis is a powerful therapy and should never be attempted unless under the direction of a trained professional.

I feel that hypnosis has its place in the therapy of phobias, but only a very small portion of people would need to avail themselves of this type of therapy. Most people displaying a fear reaction would benefit more from the phobia reduction program, whereby they take the reponsibility for the treatment processes themselves. Success becomes theirs and they learn to take the responsibility for any failures. Through the process of self-directed systematic therapy, the patient increases his or her chances for emotional growth and development.

FLOODING

This technique should only be used by specially-trained therapists and involves a considerable amount of time and special organization. The procedure consists of evoking very strong responses to stressful situations, either by imaginary or real-life situations.

An example of this procedure might involve a woman who had a phobia towards spiders. She would be placed in a room, and numerous harmless spiders let loose on the floor. She would be forced to remain in the room as her fear continued to increase. Soon this fear would reach panic proportions and then gradually subside as the therapist instructed her to keep calm and not to panic.

However, flooding does not always work, as the following example illustrates, and can, indeed, create an increase in the phobic response.

> Linda was a very pleasant fifty-three-year-old woman. She reported that spiders had always caused her a certain amount of fear but recently the phobia had increased immensely. As a child, she remembered being deathly afraid of spiders and running out of the bathroom screaming at the sight of even the smallest one. Other children who knew of her fear were always teasing her about spiders and small boys her own age were quick to pick up on the game of teasing Linda about spiders. Rather than suffer through the humiliation and constant teasing of her playmates, Linda never again mentioned her fear of spiders.
>
> Throughout her life, she kept this fear hidden away and developed elaborate excuses and avoidance mechanisms to keep her away from areas which might harbor spiders or spider webs.
>
> Finally, she confided in her husband who began a process of trying to reassure her that the spiders were relatively harmless. He would buy books showing pictures of spiders, picking out the ones that were completely harmless and noting how very few species are harmful.
>
> These did nothing to relieve Linda's fear. If anything, her fear increased whenever she knew he was going to discuss spiders. He had read in a book somewhere that forcing a person to confront the object of their fear will help them get rid of that reaction. So he went out and bought a small tarantula at the pet store and brought it home for her to look at. Right after that Linda came to see me for

therapy. Although the tarantula was perfectly harmless, Linda had a severe phobic reaction which was accompanied by a rash and inability to sleep.

Her husband's intentions were good, but he was proceeding in the wrong manner. His "flooding" technique was not working.

I met with Linda for one session and we discussed the problem fully. As she said: "I've lived with this fear for so long, and I'm so tired of it, I'd do almost anything to overcome my fear. I'm just plain tired of being scared of spiders."

I felt that since the husband had been involved previously, he could play an active role in her treatment. The next time Linda was accompanied by her husband and I explained the phobia reduction program to both of them. She was given the self-report questionnaires and instructed to fill them out. I explained the transcripts for the relaxation process and it was decided that her husband would record the relaxation procedures for her. They both agreed that working together would be the best approach. I reinforced this and told them to check back with me in one week, to insure that the process was progressing adequately.

In one week, Linda called me on the telephone to tell me that a follow-up visit was not necessary and that she had obtained tremendous results from the entire procedure. She reported some resistance at first to her husband's voice, but this soon passed. She was not at the point yet where she could confront live spiders but hearing about spiders and seeing pictures of spiders no longer elicited the chronic fear reaction as before.

CASE

Although Dennis was in his early 30's, he had been afraid of the dark since he experienced night time combat duty while serving in the army in Vietnam. I decided to use flooding in his case, to help him overcome the fear of darkness. In my center, I have a large therapy room which can be made completely dark. I told Dennis what was going to happen and had him sit in the middle of the room in a chair. All furniture which could cause any harm was removed. I left the room, turning out the light as I went. Immediately Dennis began to panic and searched for the light switch. The room has an external switch and so Dennis was not able to turn on the lights. His panic gradually mounted and I could hear him yelling for me to turn on the light. As had been agreed previously, I ignored his calling and did not turn on the lights. We had developed a behavioral contract which stated clearly that he would stay in the room for a period of four minutes and under no circumstances was I to turn on the lights unless his physical well-being was endangered. After two minutes, Dennis' yelling subsided and he began to practice his relaxation-autogenic techniques.

The panic had reached its high point and now Dennis was able to look at his behavior rationally while in the confines of the dark room. The therapy was quite successful in his case and Dennis' phobic reaction to darkened rooms was extinguished after only three more sessions.

THE USE OF BIOFEEDBACK FOR PHOBIA REDUCTION

The word biofeedback has recently become one of the most publicized treatments known to the general public. Articles in magazines from *Reader's Digest* to *Playboy* have cited the new and intriguing field of biofeedback research therapy. Dr. Barbara Brown has had several best-selling books dealing with biofeedback and its use. Most major institutions of higher learning in the Unites States are embarking upon research in biofeedback.

Biofeedback can be divided into several areas. The name itself tells us that we are going to be getting feedback on some biological or body process. The basic premise of biofeedback is that if we are provided with a measure of events happening within our body, we will eventually be able to control them. This involves gaining control over certain aspects of the autonomic nervous system, which until only recently was thought to be out of the realm of man's conscious control.

Biofeedback machines are designed to measure a variety of body responses. Due to miniaturization and sophisticated electronic processing, these machines are completely portable and their reliability is good to excellent. Thermal biofeedback, which is used to regulate blood flow within the body, has proven quite

effective in the reduction of migraine headaches and some circulatory diseases. EEG biofeedback (electroencephalographic ·
biofeedback) of the brain waves has been used in the control of
pain and to enhance the production of alpha brain waves, which
are associated with a state of relaxation. GSR biofeedback (gal-
vanic skin resistance), which is a measure of perspiration, has
been used to help induce states of relaxation. And muscle tension
or electromyographic (EMG) biofeedback has been most effective in reducing muscle tension headache. Some of the principles
of biofeedback have been integrated into the lie detector, which
measures autonomic body responses.

With the advent of biofeedback, more people will be able to
deceive a polygraph or lie detector. The lie detector was based on
the assumption that an individual is unable to control his autonomic nervous system and therefore unable to deceive the
machine. In numerous cases, we found this assumption to be
false.

Electromyographic biofeedback of muscle contraction can be
combined with the desensitization process in phobia reduction.
The use of this form of biofeedback can be a very productive
adjunctive therapy to help the patient learn the relaxation-
autogenic procedures. After these skills are learned, the machine
can then serve as an objective measurement of the patient's
progress in keeping muscles relaxed. In my own practice, I have
found that EMG biofeedback is very useful for people who have
trouble relaxing and for those people who experience difficulties
in the imagery process of the hierarchy. The major drawbacks to
biofeedback are that relaxation must be done under the guidance
of a therapist and that the patient could become too dependent
upon the machine and lazy about developing his own system of
relaxation-autogenics.

DRUG TREATMENT FOR PHOBIAS

The intention of this book is to enable readers to develop their
own program to reduce phobic reactions. When these phobic

reactions are diminished, fear and anxiety response mechanisms will also be reduced.

Drugs have long been used to treat fear and anxiety arising out of phobic reactions. However, the therapeutic value of these medications is only in treating the symptoms and not in treating the underlying disorder. Appropriate attention must always be given to the reason for the phobic reaction. Treating the symptom will essentially not change the cause for the fear. When the medication is withdrawn, the phobic response will, in all likelihood, return in full force.

In many cases, the fear and anxiety response causes uncomfortable body changes and these may be treated directly, such as controlling diarrhea with diphenoxylate (Lomotil) or nausea with Compazine.

Many doctors have used sedatives for the treatment of anxiety induced by a phobic reaction. These sedatives are the so-called minor tranquilizers — chlordiazepoxide (Librium), diazepam (Valium), and meprobamate (Miltown, Equanil). Many physicians make a distinction and prefer to use a major tranquilizer, such as a phenothiazine or butyrophenone, when the fear and anxiety is severe or when some form of brain disorder is suspected. It should be pointed out that there is no connection between phobic reactions and brain disease.

The tranquilizers and sedatives used today can relieve certain symptoms. But there are significant drawbacks to the continued use of medication to relieve symptoms due to an underlying psychological problem. As a professional who deals with people displaying minor to extremely severe psychological problems, it is obvious that some severe psychotic and schizophrenic disorders do definitely benefit from the use of appropriate drugs. There are also a considerable number of people with relatively minor psychological tension, anxiety, fear-related reactions, who are being over-medicated. Treating the symptom and covering the actual cause of the problem is not the only adverse effect related to taking medications of a psychotropic nature.

Mr. B. was a 28-year-old married man with two young children. He was referred to me with symptoms of dizziness, increased anxiety and headaches. He also reported an inability to concentrate and recurring nightmares. Upon further examination, I found that the patient was suffering from "night terrors" and not simply nightmares. Nightmares may be disquieting events during sleep, but night terrors are usually found after a traumatic experience. The patient reports that brief frightening images intrude upon the normal flow of dreaming. Normally, nightmares are disturbing events during sleep which occur very quickly and do not persist over a long period of time. A person suffering from night terrors will experience profuse sweating, accelerated heart rate up to 150 to 170 beats per minute and extreme psychomotor agitation (jerking and spasm of the arms and legs, cramping of the muscles). Numerous patients have also reported that while suffering "night terrors," there will be verbal agitation such as moans, loud exclamations and a sensation of terror. Research indicates that night terrors, unlike nightmares, may occur during stages III and IV of the normal sleep pattern. Nightmares have usually been found to take place during the REM (Rapid Eye Movement) stage of sleep.

When Mr. B. came to me, he had already completed an extensive neurological and neuropsychiatric evaluation. No specific neurological signs or evidence of organic brain damage were revealed. The patient's records showed no previous psychiatric episodes. Mr. B. had previously received treatment for his symptoms from several physicians. Treatment included the usual variety of psychotropic drugs used for the symptomatic control of anxiety — including phenobarbitol, meprobamate and diazepam.

A thorough examination of this patient's records revealed that although he had not had any major hospitalizations, eight months before he had experienced severe chest pain radiating into the left arm. After being examined by a cardiologist and receiving a stress EKG, Mr. B. was found to have no heart problem. I found it to be more than a coincidence that this patient's night terrors had begun immediately following the evaluation by the cardiologist.

He was questioned about this matter and confirmed that he had never experienced night terrors prior to his testing. My conclusion was that this individual was suffering from a post-traumatic phobic reaction. Evidently the fear and trauma elicited by the thought of a possible heart condition had produced a traumatic phobic reaction. Since the use of medications had not proven useful and there was no sign of organic dysfunction, he had been referred to me for treatment of his post-traumatic phobic reaction. It was evident that during the time of the examination by the cardiologist, the patient was extremely frightened and feared that he might die at a very young age. This fear was transferred into a generalized phobic reaction. The headaches, dizziness, and weakness in the arms and legs occurred when the patient was a passenger in automobiles or planes. Any discussion of accidents or illness also generated these disturbing symptoms.

His statement at the end of our first session typifies the anxiety experienced by patients suffering from a post-traumatic phobic reaction.

"You've got to help me, Doctor. I hate taking those drugs. They make me feel better riding in a car and I don't worry so much about accidents, but they don't seem to get rid of those horrible dreams. I can't go on like this for the rest of my life. Something has to be done."

The patient's pleading for help indicated that his symptoms would most likely continue to worsen if he were not taught to gain control over his fear. Mr. B. reported that so far the problems had not affected his job, but that if they got any worse he didn't know how long it would be before he was fired.

After taking the fear inventory, it was found that this patient had the following fears, in order of intensity:

(1) fear of death, (2) fear of injury, (3) fear of nightmares.

Mr. B. constructed a hierarchy for the fear of nightmares and this was placed on an audiotape. Simultaneously, the patient was instructed in relaxation-autogenic procedures.

After explaining the process to him completely, he did express a concern that all his phobic reactions and obsessional behaviors were not being worked on at the same time. I explained to him that we needed to start with the least fear-producing of his phobic reactions and if we could successfully stop this behavior, then it would be much easier to conquer the more distressing phobias.

It took Mr. B. almost three and a half months to work through all his phobic reactions. During that time, he was subject to some discouragement and had to be reinforced and instructed to practice more often.

His situation was not uncommon, in that many people who gain successes with this treatment procedure will begin to practice slightly less each day. His sessions had gone from three 15 to 20 minute sessions a day to one session in the morning. After I had checked his progress and found he was not practicing enough, his program was increased to four times a day. When he followed through with this practice regimen, the total phobia reduction process was enhanced.

During the three and a half months I saw him only for recheck purposes and during this time he reported a definite improvement in his sense of well-being and a decrease in frustration and irritability. Before the treatment sessions, he had noticed increasing fatigue during his work day activities, but now he became aware of less fatigue and more motivation.

One aspect of the phobic reaction which had not been covered previously was a decrease in his sexual functioning during the time of "night terrors." Lack of sexual interest is not uncommon during a post-traumatic phobic reaction. A return to normal sexual activity appeared to be one of the side benefits of the phobia reduction program.

This case study brings up several points which are extremely important to people who have suffered from phobic reactions. One of the most important is the fact that many drugs which are used in the treatment of anxiety only tend to mask the cause of the problem. As with Mr. B., when the drug was withdrawn, the symptoms returned. I have noticed in many patients who have previously tried a course of antidepressant or anti-anxiety medication, that while they are on the medication and receive some form of relief, this false sense of cure may cause them to experience an increase in symptoms once they are taken off the medication. This increase in symptoms may be due in part to the psychological readjustment to a return of the phobic reaction.

THE PROBLEM OF SYMPTOM SUBSTITUTION:

On occasion, I have been queried by physicians as to the frequency of "symptom substitution." Symptom substitution is best explained by the following example.

Don was a 34-year-old school teacher who made an appointment with me for hypnosis to help him quit smoking. We proceeded with the hypnosis treatment and after three sessions, the patient did not smoke for eight weeks. After eight weeks he contacted me as instructed to report his progress. He said he had not smoked one single cigarette during that period of time.

The patient was again checked after four months and he reported that he still was not smoking, but was quite upset about a nine-pound weight gain. I called him in and we discussed the matter. Since he had smoked mostly during times of nervousness and tension, he had replaced cigarette smoking with eating. He was devouring anything from candy bars to donuts at a very unhealthy rate. I asked him why he had not mentioned this problem sooner and he said he was embarrassed and did not think it would amount to much of anything.

This example points to the problem of symptom substitution. His smoking was a symptom of an inability to control tension and stress during the work day. Hypnosis treated the one symptom and when this symptom was diminished, another took its place. The patient now realized that he should have been more honest about the reasons for his smoking habit. We immediately embarked upon a relaxation-autogenic training program to reverse his maladaptive reaction to stress situations.

A follow-up report indicated that the patient still was not smoking and the substitute symptom of eating had also been extinguished. He reported that his work performance had increased and stressful situations no longer triggered an anxiety reaction.

Researchers and experts in the field of fear have long sought answers to the questions of symptom substitution. Despite fears of symptom substitution, follow-up of phobic patients treated by behavior therapy has shown that successful treatment is not marked by replacement with new symptoms. In fact, quite the reverse is often true.

I have found in my practice that the use of phobia reduction programs may trigger clinical improvements in other areas of social adjustment. It would be impossible to predict how the reduction of a phobic response will affect the generalized behavior of an individual. The one thing we know for sure is that the effect will be a positive one. We spend a good portion of our lives concealing anxieties and small fears. When I have someone go through the phobia reduction program for a major phobia, sometimes minor fears which have persisted during the individual's lifetime are simultaneously released and resolved.

For this reason, I explain to patients that there is a need to practice the relaxation-autogenic training throughout their entire lifetime. By using this procedure to reduce anxiety and fear responses, it can serve as a lifetime therapy.

Once you make it a habit, systematic phobia reduction will be a positive influence on all aspects of your behavior. Life will become more productive, and at the same time, more enjoyable.

CHAPTER NINE
It Could Happen to You

> *"What governs men is the fear of truth."*
>
> HENRI FREDERIC AMIEL:
> Journal, March 1, 1869.

In a society fraught with compulsions and obsessions to earn more money, obtain a higher position, get a bigger house, and gain more status, it is little wonder that many people suffer from a fear of failure. This phobic reaction towards failure seems to be implanted early in our lives and is nurtured by ever-increasing pressures to achieve more and more.

We are constantly reminded of the effects of failure by people who commit suicide after a business setback or commit crimes to cover failure. More commonly, untold numbers of people will not extend themselves for fear of failing.

An integral part of the fear of failure is the fear of becoming a failure in the eyes of relatives, family and others whose opinion we care about. We may avoid a task for fear of failing and thereby hope to maintain the good impression others have of us.

Avoiding situations which might produce failure can become obsessional. An obsessional idea soon occupies a large part of the individual's thinking. The more he concentrates on avoiding the situation, the more his symptoms of fear increase. As we can see from the diagram, pretty soon a fully-fledged phobia develops.

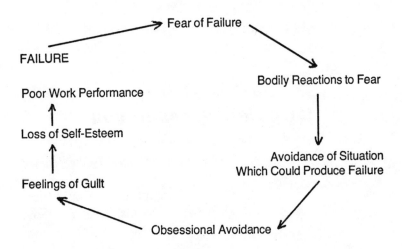

As the circle closes, the individual experiences intense phobic reaction symptoms and sets himself up for the failure he so arduously tries to avoid.

In today's society, the fear of failure appears to strike at men and women who are in positions of high responsibility and authority. As more women have been entering stressful jobs in industry and government, this type of phobia has become increasingly common among women in the past few years.

The following case will illustrate the effects of chronic phobic reaction towards failure in a 35-year-old woman.

Betty had been employed by a local department store for nine years. She had served as a sales girl and worked her way up to assistant department manager. The store put all department managers through a management training program, and in the past this had been essentially limited to men. Only women's clothing and cosmetics were under the control of a female manager.

As the assistant manager in the cosmetics department, Betty was given the chance to participate in a six-month management trainee program. She took the course and did extremely well, placing fifth in a class of 15 management trainees.

At the completion of the course, she was transferred to another store across town and assumed the role of probationary manager of the cosmetics department. This probation period was to last nine months. At the end of that time, if her work performance was satisfactory, she would then be given the role of permanent department manager.

Since Betty was single, she began to devote more and more time to the store. She experienced a certain amount of natural nervousness and anxiety as she assumed her new duties. After the first month, however, she became increasingly aware of her obsessional need to be in the store at every minute, and watch over her staff.

Betty became worried that other people were watching her and that people in management were looking for a chance to knock her out of the job. Along with this increase in anxiety and obsessional behavior, Betty noticed that she was spending more time drinking her lunches and frequenting cocktail lounges after work. Liquor appeared to be the only thing that could help her settle down, and many nights she would fall asleep in an alcohol-laced exhaustion. She seemed to be getting fewer tasks accomplished, yet expending more and more energy daily. After three and one-half months in this new position, most of her friends would not have recognized her. In fact, she had lost several close friends due to the fact that she had no time for anything other than her job at the store.

This is a very clear-cut case of an individual who had such a fear of failure that she was actively participating in her own downfall.

The harder she tried to work, the poorer the results.

Betty was even becoming paranoid whenever the assistant store manager came through her department. Every time she saw him she was sure he was going to tell her that her work was inadequate and that she would have to go back to being a salesperson. Because of this paranoia, Betty began to avoid him and many of the management personnel of the store.

In the fourth month of her probationary period, Betty had to be told of some procedures which she was not performing adequately. This was combined with a standard work performance critique, which was always held in the fourth month of the management probationary period. The day of the evaluation Betty awoke with nausea, fatigue, a feeling of light-headedness and a headache, which throbbed and pounded relentlessly. She took several aspirin and tried to calm herself down. After several hours the symptoms persisted and she called into work sick.

She had no appetite and remained in a semi-listless state for two to three days. On the third day, she called the store physician and made an appointment to see him.

By the time she saw him that afternoon, she had lost most of her desire to do anything and her physical symptoms were becoming worse. The dizziness and blurry vision were now present all the time.

This woman's doctor, with whom I had worked before, quickly recognized the symptoms of her phobic reaction. His physical examination revealed that there were no organic problems. She was not eating well due to her increased intake of alcohol and had become slightly anemic. This condition was corrected with some supplemental shots and by putting her on a regimen of vitamins. The medical treatment only touched a portion of her problem, however. Even with medical advice and vitamin supplements, it was clear that unless she rid herself of her phobia she would continue to worsen. She was now precariously close to losing her position as a probationary manager.

At the physician's request, I talked with her, and in the beginning she was resistant to the idea of a phobic reaction to failure. She assured me that in no way was she scared of failure and in fact in her own opinion her behavior was related to extreme self-confidence. She listened attentively as I told her my opinion — that her obsessive need for success had generated a phobic reaction towards failure. She was extremely fearful of failure and therefore had developed all of the somatic [bodily] responses that accompany an acute phobic reaction. At the same time, she was fearful of the responsibilities ultimately to be placed upon her if she was successful. These two conflicting emotions caused an increase in her level of fear. The fear and anxiety could not help but cause her to suffer physically.

My preliminary attempts to explain the connection between fear and her body response appeared to fall upon deaf ears. She did ask that I send her the phobia reduction program, however, and she said she would look it over and make a decision in the next week.

I was extremely concerned that she would continue to deny the relationship between the reaction to her job and her present physical condition. Any delay at this time would prolong the time needed for the phobia reduction program to work. Each day that went by was time that she could profitably be using to start Phase I of the program.

I was extremely gratified and very surprised to hear from her within two days. My statements had stuck in her mind and she had thought about them over and over again. After she received the program, and had read the introduction, she decided that there might be some validity to my statements. Taking the fear index and identifying her phobic reactions reinforced her now growing belief that she actually was extremely fearful of failure and in the process of developing a fear of success. She was now painfully aware that with these two phobias working against her she would quickly be sent back to her former job as a salesgirl. She told me she would start the program immediately and I asked her to call in a week.

One week exactly from the day on which I had talked to her, she called. The first two phases of the program were completed and she was now proceeding with the desensitization process. Although she had only just started desensitization, she could already notice changes in her behavior as she used the relaxation procedures to combat her fear and anxiety while on the job. She had set aside certain times during the day to practice the program.

Even as I talked to her, I could hear a new strength and resolution in her voice. There was a definite tone of authority and I felt confident that she would be able to continue the phobia reduction program to a happy conclusion.

I did not hear from this patient for approximately one year. I made no inquiries as to her final disposition. It was not until one Saturday afternoon, when shopping with my wife, that I felt a tap on my shoulder. I turned around and found myself face to face with a woman who wore the badge of manager of the cosmetics department. She only smiled back at me and said nothing. The uncomfortable silence was very confusing to me until I connected the name with the referral from the department store doctor.

The badge had answered my question. After the introductions were made, she went on to tell me it had been a very difficult uphill battle, but had been worth it in the end.

Later, she had used the same program to overcome her long-standing fear of flying. So far, she felt her fear of flying was gradually diminishing. The true test would come in a month, when she hoped to fulfill a life-long dream and fly to Hawaii for her summer vacation.

In my experience, many people who use the phobia reduction program successfully continue to use it for other phobias which they had not planned to work with in the beginning. The increased confidence in their ability to solve their own fear increases their commitment towards self-initiated positive change.

DENTAL PHOBIA

An increasingly common phobia is that of the fear of having dental work performed. A recent national survey showed that over 50 percent of the population does not visit a dentist regularly; over 14 percent of those surveyed list fear as the primary reason for avoiding the dentist. This means that millions of people are neglecting their teeth due to a phobia of dental work.

Information gained from the report indicated that people who had a dental phobia acquired this through a traumatic personal experience or vicariously, from family or friends. Many of these people reported traumatic experiences early in childhood. They remembered the dentist as someone who caused them discomfort.

Elliott came to me with a severe dental phobia. He was in his late 20's and needed to have two wisdom teeth removed. The condition had become quite painful and his dentist insisted on oral surgery. His fear of having his wisdom teeth removed was strong enough for him to endure continuous discomfort with possible damage to the other teeth.

During my initial interview with him, he explained that as a young boy his father had had several teeth removed. He developed what is called a "dry socket" and required numerous trips to the dentist. His father continuously complained of the discomfort. Furthermore, his son was present on several occasions when the father would rinse out his mouth and spit blood into the sink. These vivid impressions and the modeling behavior of his father precipitated a severe phobia in Elliott towards having his wisdom teeth removed.

Elliott could rationally acknowledge that his teeth needed to be taken out, but fear held him back. When he came to me, his wisdom teeth were close to becoming impacted and the more the pain increased, the greater the fear reaction grew.

Elliott was anxious to overcome the phobia and we began work immediately. Since the time was very short, I used hypnosis to induce immediate deep muscle relaxation. While in the hypnotic state, I provided Elliott with instructions for the relaxation-autogenic training exercises. Although I do not use this method in all cases, the medical necessity in Elliott's case warranted the technique. Within four days, Elliott was able to progress completely through the hierarchy relating to the extraction of his teeth. He had first come to me on Monday and the following Friday, Elliott had his teeth extracted.

Unfortunately, many people are not as lucky as Elliott. He had a desire to resolve the problem and took action. Poor dental care is a growing problem within our society and the phobic reaction towards dentistry is definitely impeding the development of better dental habits for large numbers of people.

Take a moment to examine your own behavior towards dental treatment. If you have children, analyze your reaction to the dentist and see if you are providing a modeling behavior for your children which would lead them to develop a dental phobia. Your behavior towards dentists may be influencing your children or, if you do not have any, you may be assisting in the development of this type of reaction in a friend or relative.

Dental schools are now instructing dental students in methods for reducing fear and anxiety in patients. This is a great step forward but first you must overcome your fear in order to get into the dentist's office. Once this happens, a properly trained dentist will be able to provide you with positive suggestions to make your dental treatment less anxiety-provoking.

FEAR OF CRIME

Recent studies have shown that the fear of crime will affect the lives of eight out of ten citizens of the United States during their lifetime. Most researchers tend to agree that the development of a phobic reaction towards crime is not necessarily the result of direct exposure as a victim.

J. E. Conklin (1971) has distinguished between "direct victimization" (the experience of the victim in such crimes as attempted murder, rape, robbery and burglary) and "indirect victimization," in which an individual may suffer a loss from a crime in which he is not directly involved, such as a robbery taking place while he is away from home.

As the owner of a small convenience market, Jack had very little fear of crime until he had been robbed three times in a period of one and one-half months. Each time the robber carried a gun. During the last robbery, Jack was severely beaten about the head with a pistol.

After his recovery, he found that he was phobic about being in the store alone at night. Since his store was located in a rural community, he tried to install new security measures, but because the store was isolated these were relatively ineffective. The feeling of isolation and the dread of further robberies increased his victimization phobia.

Jack was in his late forties and had owned the convenience market for eleven years. Although he and his wife had no children, they did not wish to relocate. Thus they began to close the shop earlier and earlier each evening and became so distrustful of any unfamiliar person walking into the store that their suspicious behavior caused customers to go elsewhere.

Numerous sleepless nights and constantly being on the alert for something happening in the store gradually took its toll on Jack's health. The fear of further robberies was now affecting every part of his and his wife's lives.

As the extreme phobic reaction continued to take its toll, Jack suffered a "mental breakdown" and his wife subsequently divorced him. Jack became an outpatient at a local hospital. Although no phobia reduction program could have prevented the robberies, if a program had been made available to him immediately after the incidents, Jack may not have developed such an extreme fear response.

Since no one can predict when a crime is going to occur, phobia reduction is limited in its ability to prevent fear in those who may become victims. While younger people are usually mobile in their jobs, residence and means of transportation, and can escape crime-ridden areas, the same does not hold true for the elderly. For them, the fear of victimization is a very real and pervasive fact of life. Many elderly people will not leave their homes for fear of crime. Our studies have shown that when elderly people live in a homogenous setting, among people of their own age, sympathetic and supportive relationships will develop. These relationships tend to decrease the fear quotient and we find less phobic reactions developing. In contrast, the aged who live alone or in a mixed neighborhood, tend to feel the impact of phobic reactions towards crime more intensely than other elderly groups. Many spend their lives hidden away from the reality of day-to-day life.

Goldsmith and Thomas (1974), have stated the elderly's plight very graphically:

". . . criminal behavior has a chilling effect upon the freedom of older Americans. Fear of victimization causes self-imposed 'house arrest' among older people. . . ."

Fear of crime among the elderly is a harsh reality and the need for some type of therapeutic intervention to reduce these acute and chronic phobic reactions is definitely needed.

The answer to crime in America does not lie solely in the

reduction of the fear reaction, but a program such as the one outlined in this book can go a long way towards reducing the side effects produced by the devastating reality of victimization.

When dealing with a wide portion of the population, different factors affect the development of the fear response towards crime. These factors can be broken down into: (1) sex, (2) socio-economic status, (3) race, and (4) size of the community.

Men of all age groups are less likely to report fear reactions than women, although this response pattern appears to diminish somewhat in elderly men. The reluctance of men to admit to fear of crime can be directly related to the socialization process of our society. Men are taught to be strong, fearless and maintain a "knight in shining armor" image.

A recent report by Clemente and Kleiman found that blacks reported a consistently higher fear of crime than whites. These figures appear to hold true for blacks of all ages, but was significantly more evident among the aged. Their data showed that less than one-half of the white elderly respondents expressed fear, while over two-thirds of the black elderly reported that they were afraid to walk in their neighborhoods alone at night.

Common sense will tell us that people in the higher socio-economic levels generally feel less fear of crime than people of the lower economic levels. This assumption was born out by the research of Ennis, 1967, along with follow-up studies by other researchers who found that income was a more significant factor for the young than the elderly. Education did not seem to provide any significant differences between the different age categories.

Community size also plays an important role in the level of fear among different age groups. As might be expected, residents of larger, more congested cities had a higher reported fear index than did those living in rural areas or smaller towns. Elderly residents of cities with a population over 50,000 tend to display a significantly higher fear index of crime than the young. In the larger cities, it is not uncommon to find people of all age groups displaying fear of strangers, increased anxiety when approached by several young people on the street and fright and fear when in dimly lit areas, such as elevators and streets. Residents of the larger cities tend to be those who display the "house arrest" syndrome. Rose, who lived in New York City, was an example of this syndrome. She had resided in a small frame apartment for fifteen years. Before her husband's death he had worked in the garment industry and Rose now lived off the small social security and pension money she received each month. Although Rose was nearing her 67th birthday, she remained very active in various volunteer organizations and was seldom found in her apartment. Her neighbors could always count on her to take long walks, no matter what the weather.

One day Rose finished work early at the Children's Hospital and was walking home by her usual route. Along the way, she acknowledged the friendly hellos of people who had known her for many, many years.

Two blocks away from her house, while turning the corner, she was knocked to the street and her purse was stolen by a youth who kicked her in the side of the head before fleeing. She suffered a broken hip and her jaw was fractured in two places.

The recovery was long and painful. Bones heal slowly at that age. No one noticed anything significantly different in her behavior during the recovery. She was somewhat depressed and quiet, but that was to be expected after suffering such an attack.

The orthopedic surgeon who treated her for the injuries became aware of the emotional after-effects during her follow-up visits. His concern grew as she became more isolated and withdrawn.

A short trial of some mild antidepressant medication proved to be ineffective. Rose had now confined herself to the "house arrest" lifestyle. Longstanding friendships were broken and contact grew less frequent with her close friends. Most people around her did not know how to deal with her sudden change in behavior and were sympathetic at first. But after a while, they decided that the difficulty they experienced in continuing a relationship with Rose was not worth the effort.

One avoidance behavior led to another and very soon Rose had built an elaborate defense mechanism to protect her physical and emotional well-being. No one entered her domain and she did not venture outside the walls she had created.

The massive fear, growing out of the attack, consumed and destroyed all the previously worthwhile aspects of this woman's life.

Through several referral mechanisms, I received a call from her orthopedic surgeon who explained the situation to me. I told him that the problem of her mental and emotional health needed to be resolved as quickly as possible. As the physician described her latest behaviors to me, I became aware that Rose was now becoming slightly delusional and developing many of the psychotic behaviors of inpatients at mental institutions. Therapy needed to be initiated immediately if the web of fear responses was to be reversed.

I started by outlining a treatment program, to be administered by a colleague of mine in New York. The therapy would be coordinated by the orthopedic surgeon. As I put the envelope in the mailbox, I was confident that we could help Rose overcome her phobias.

That afternoon I received a call from Rose's orthopedic surgeon. He told me not to bother mailing the information for he had just received word that early the same morning Rose had jumped from her third story window and died instantly.

Throughout this book, I have given you many case studies and the subsequent treatment program. Although Rose never did benefit from treatment, I have included her story to illustrate the fact that if phobic reactions and fear responses are not diminished, they can become so severe as to cause mental imbalance.

To Rose, the two things which she feared the most, injury and death, eventually became her only mechanism of escape. No one can guarantee the results of any type of treatment, but I am fairly confident that we could have reversed many of the effects of Rose's disability and therefore extinguished many of the responses that led to her suicide.

What happened to Rose may be happening to countless numbers of elderly citizens around the United States. Not all the cases are as severe, but national statistics bear out the ugly facts that very little is provided the aged to help them overcome fear of crime. With increasing violence on television, the fear of physical injury brought about by crime slowly pervades all age brackets. Exposure to violence on television, the movies and magazines may reinforce both violence and the fear of crime. At this very moment, many national, state and local agencies are making concerted efforts to diminish the impact of crime upon the victim and the population in general. The thrust towards resolution of this problem is multi-faceted and reduction of the fear response should be considered a prime element of these efforts.

Among women, fear of rape is one of the most terrifying aspects of living and working in a large city.

Susan was the mother of three and, from all appearances, had a good solid marriage. Her husband was a lawyer and maintained a thriving private practice within the city. Before the night of January 23, she reported that nothing in particular scared her and that life was very normal.

On that night, Susan left for the supermarket at 8 o'clock in the evening. After shopping for a half hour, she returned to her car. While she fumbled for her keys, two men jumped on her, dragged her behind an apartment building and raped her. The police were brought into the case and both men were apprehended. After a long and, for Susan, a very emotionally painful trial, both men were convicted.

Immediately after the incident, Susan was helped by the Crisis Intervention workers from the police department and sought psychiatric help. During the time of the trial, her husband did not attempt sexual intercourse, as the doctor had told him she would require a period of adjustment.

Soon the adjustment period stretched to two months, then three. Finally, after six months her husband began to worry when his previously very affectionate wife rejected all his attempts at sexual relations. Her excuses were varied and at this point he sought a consultation with her psychiatrist, whom she had not seen for approximately two months.

The psychiatrist told him that Susan had probably developed a very understandable fear towards intercourse and although they had experienced a loving relationship before, she was now transferring the trauma and anguish of that night to any sexual relationship.

They tried to talk about it, but she became very agitated and disturbed when approached about sexual relations. Soon afterwards, she stopped talking about sex altogether and both of them realized that their once stable marriage was beginning to crumble.

The husband and wife were referred to my practice by their psychiatrist. He knew I had specialized in phobia reduction and felt that therapy with me would be helpful.

I met with them, and although it was very painful, I had her bring me completely up-to-date about her feelings towards sex. It was quite obvious that she had developed a phobic reaction towards sexual intercourse due to the trauma of the rape. I felt that the phobic reduction regimen would be warranted in this case. Since her husband was actively involved in trying to help her, I had him record the relaxation exercises and autogenic training on a cassette tape recorder. His wife was to train with this tape. The training was thus made easier for her and the relaxation was immediately associated with her husband's presence through his voice. She went through the desensitization process by constructing her own hierarchy of fear (with her husband's help) towards sexual relations.

Constructing this hierarchy was extremely painful and took longer than most to construct. She checked the hierarchy against several examples which I had provided and then began the desensitization process. After proceeding with desensitization with satisfactory results, she and her husband then went through the hierarchy "in vivo" and found that she was able to have sexual intercourse with only minimal anxiety and fear. They continued to practice this method, using the relaxation and desensitization process frequently and after two months reported that their relationship was the way it had been before the incident and that they now felt closer than ever before.

This is a good example of the marriage partner helping the phobic individual resolve the fear reaction. If two people are able to work together closely in this manner, then the results are often more productive than if an individual works on his or her own.

Not all the people I treat come through referral from other physicians. As the police psychologist for a local law enforcement agency, I was summoned to interview a man in his early 30's who had been arrested the night before. When I arrived at the station, the duty sergeant briefed me on the particulars.

"His name is Harry Bennett, which we have verified through his driver's license and other identification. He was apprehended after midnight by one of our patrol officers, who spotted him entering a residence through the side window." The sergeant chuckled as he continued the story. "Our officers apprehended him without incident and informed him of his rights. Mr. Bennett then insisted that the house was owned by a friend of his who was on vacation, and that he had been put in charge of checking the interior every two or three days."

So far, I was curious as to why I had been brought in on the case. "Why do you need me? It seems like a pretty clear-cut case of breaking and entering," I asked.

"That's what we all thought until we verified with the owner of the house that Mr. Bennett was left with the responsibility of checking the interior. The owner had even left him with a key to the front door."

Getting more confused by the minute, I asked my next question: "Did he forget the key and have to try to get in through the window?"

The sergeant who had been on the police force for over fifteen years, placed both his hands, palm down, on the table, looked me straight in the eye and said, "That's what's so strange; we found the house key in his pocket and he insists that he cannot go through doors to houses, cars, or anything.''

"Any doors?''

"That's what he said and you should have seen the battle we had trying to get him into the car. He insisted that he wanted to go through the window.''

I had to ask the next question. "How did you get him into the station?'' "By the time we got him to the station, he was hysterical and fighting like a bear. One of the officers had to mace him to keep him quiet.''

"*Any* doors?''

"That's what he says, any doors.

"The reason why we called you, Doc, is that he insisted that it is a psychological problem and that he cannot go through doors. He wanted us to have a psychologist see him.''

The sergeant handed me the arrest folder and I thumbed through it on my way to seeing Mr. Bennett. As it turned out, Mr. Bennett was a very pleasant 36-year-old man who had been under therapy for three years before moving to Arizona. Since he had been in Arizona, he had not sought any professional help for his phobia. He provided me with the name of his psychiatrist in New Jersey and after several phone calls, I verified that he had been treated for a phobic reaction to doorways.

As it turned out, Mr. Bennett had an extreme phobic reaction to any types of doorways. This meant he entered and exited his house through a window and he drove a small Volkswagen convertible, which afforded him the ability to hop over the door and into the car. He would not ride in airplanes, nor would he enter public buildings because of this phobic reaction. He told me that the psychiatrist had tried hypnosis at one time about two years before and that it had worked for two or three weeks. Mr. Bennett worked for a local lawn service and therefore was not required to go indoors during his work day. Since he was unmarried, he could cover up much of his weird behavior. A previous marriage had dissolved due to his phobic reactions.

The police matter was cleared up fairly easily and Mr. Bennett became a patient.

Mr. Bennett was fully aware of the reason for his phobic reaction. When he was a young boy, around the age of seven, he had been following his mother through the doorway of an old house of a friend they were visiting. When she entered the doorway, several of the rafters broke and the doorway collapsed on his mother. She was severely injured and had to spend a long time recuperating in the hospital. This incident was so traumatic that Harry would not go through doorways after the incident. The overwhelming fear of almost losing his mother developed into a very severe chronic phobic reaction. Whenever forced to enter through a doorway, he would develop extreme nausea and vomiting.

This accounted for extremely poor grades in school, constantly being sent to the nurse's office and subsequently being sent to doctors for his physical problems. Tests were run for years with no doctor finding an organic reason for his difficulties. Finally he was sent to a psychiatrist who, upon delving into his past, rooted out the cause of his phobic reaction.

I explained to Mr. Bennett the cause of his reaction and how, through the home practice program, he could overcome the fear of doorways. He realized it was a silly thing to be afraid of, but no amount of talking or explaining could help him get rid of the anxiety and fear reaction. I gave him the training material, plus a set of relaxation training tapes. He proceeded through this material and was able to attain a satisfactory level of relaxation. I then had him proceed with the second step which was to develop the anxiety hierarchy at a very rapid pace, combining the relaxation response with the phobic response. I should mention at this time that most of the work was done by Mr. Bennett himself, at home.

After going through the chronic phobic reaction treatment, Mr. Bennett was able to approach and go through certain doorways. There was still some minor reaction left, mostly related to doorways of houses.

Mr. Bennett then developed a hierarchy specifically for doorways to houses and after a short period of training, was able to satisfactorily extinguish the phobic reaction.

The last word I had from Mr. Bennett was that he was now occupied as a door-to-door salesman and had no trouble entering or exiting any types of doors, including doorways to houses.

Most of my work with the police department involves people with severe and traumatic problems. Every once in a while, I am called in on a case which provides a needed change of pace from the regular police routine.

Jean was such a case. She was a woman in her middle fifties, quite pleasant and with an excellent reputation in the community. She had only one major fault — she was continually going through red lights. Her case was brought to my attention by the Justice of the Peace who was preparing to suspend her license after the fifth ticket.

The Justice told me he had a woman in the court who insisted that the color red caused her to become irrational and therefore she was not responsible for her behavior when she was driving and the light was about to turn red. I told the Judge I would need to see the woman and the court therefore required her to see me on a consultive basis for evaluation of her problems.

I was very surprised when she entered the office. I pictured a small, hardened woman who was trying to beat out some traffic tickets and was now caught by her own deceptive behavior. Instead, I was surprised to meet a slightly overweight, middle-aged woman with a smile from ear to ear. She was dressed very neatly and was extremely friendly from the very start of our meeting. Once seated in my office, I proceeded to ask her to describe the problem she brought up to the judge.

She began, "I can't stand the color red. Everytime I see a red light, I don't know what I am doing."

I could see that her hands were starting to shake and even the mention of the color red brought about physical changes.

"There is not much more to say. Every time I see a red light or a flashing red light on an ambulance, fire truck or police car, I just start to lose control. It feels as if I don't have any strength in my hands or legs and I even get spots in front of my eyes."

I motioned for her to stop at this point for she was obviously starting to become extremely upset. A few moments were spent helping her calm down, but I had to go on. "Do you have this same reaction when you are looking at a red picture in a book?"

"No."

"How about at the movies, when you see something very red, such as blood?" I wanted to see if the color red was connected with blood. I have found that in many cases where people have an aversion to a specific color, it is directly connected to a traumatic body incident.

"No. I don't get any of the same feelings when I see red on the television or newspaper. It only bothers me when I see a red light or red lights on the top of cars."

It was time to get a better picture of specific situations in which she lost control. "Tell me what you do when you are driving along and you look ahead and see a green light and it begins to turn amber."

She sat for a moment staring into the distance obviously conjuring up the scene in her mind. "When I'm driving and see green lights, there is no problem. I think I am a very good driver and except for this, I have had only one ticket. But when I see the light starting to change and I know it's going to turn red pretty soon, something tells me to speed up so I can get to the light before it turns to red."

"And that's when you get your tickets. '

"Yes."

What about the emergency vehicles? What kind of reaction do you have when you see them — let's say, out of your rear-view mirror?"

Again she looked off into the distance, but this time her hands were starting to tremble and I noticed a thin, white line above her upper lip which was an indication that she was becoming quite tense and fearful. "When I'm driving along and I hear a siren, the first thing I do is look into the rearview mirror and when I see the red lights, the same things starts to happen again.''

''Please describe them to me.''

''My hands and arms get all wobbly and shaky. It takes every bit of strength I have to pull the car over to the side of the road. I am just afraid that some day I'm going to cause a big accident and people are going to get hurt because of this.''

I reassured her that we were going to be able to work on the problem and that she would not injure anybody because of her behavior.

We spent some more time discussing her reactions to the red lights and when I asked her how long she had had this problem, she told me it was ever since her automobile accident. Her description of the incident which occurred three years before graphically illustrates the development of this woman's phobia towards the color red (erythrophobia).

She straightened herself in the chair and appeared to brace herself before beginning the story. ''It was a Wednesday or Thursday. I can't really remember now, but I was driving down Scottsdale Road and wanted to make a turn to the left. The intersection in front of me was very crowded and the light was green. I had the right of way to make a left-hand turn, when . . .'' She hesitated for a few moments before going on. ''Just as I was about to enter the intersection, the light turned yellow. I thought for sure that I could get through on the yellow, but I must have miscalculated. The light turned red all of a sudden and I was just entering the intersection and starting my turn.''

I tried to make her more comfortable, but urged her to continue her story.

''I thought for sure I had made it; I thought I had made it. All of a sudden I felt the car shudder and there was a sound of crashing, crinkling metal and glass flew everywhere. The next thing I knew, I was waking up in the hospital. I was not badly hurt and they let me go the next day with only some bumps and bruises and a couple of stitches in my head. But the other woman . . .''

''Please go on.''

"She had to stay in the hospital for three weeks. After that every time I go up to a red light, or a light that is just about to turn red, I feel this, this panic coming over me. It is like somebody grabs my throat and tries to squeeze it. It is even hard to breathe." She straightened up trying to regain her composure. "And they all think I'm crazy down at the police station. Every one of them thinks I am crazy because I said I can't stand to see red lights."

"I don't think you're crazy," I said, trying to reassure her.

She stopped for a moment thinking about my last statement, then said, "Nothing like this has ever happened to me before. I spent my life trying to be good to people and even if they didn't pay me back, that was of no consequence. I have always wanted to help people." She began to whimper quietly. "I don't know how I could have done it. I don't know how I could have done it. My foolishness caused a woman pain and suffering. I had never done that before."

Once again, we can see the connection between a traumatic incident and the development of a phobic response. The woman did not have any kind of aversion to red lights before the accident. Then she became involved in an accident where she was trying to beat a red light. People were injured and she developed a fearful response to intersections and particularly to red lights. Her fear of traffic lights became centered around the red light. It could be said that she was fearful of being put in the same situation again and having to beat the light again. She did everything to avoid the red light situation and when she could not, displayed the phobic response. Unfortunately, red lights are impossible to avoid when one drives, and so it was relatively impossible for her to avoid her phobic stimulus other than by giving up driving altogether.

In order for her to overcome this phobia effectively, it was imperative that she break the cycle and substitute a more productive response.

This patient received a cassette for relaxation training. Along with the tapes, she was given the phobia reduction program. She had no trouble in constructing the phobia hierarchy.

After successfully completing the anxiety hierarchy and going

through the most fear-producing stimulus, while remaining relaxed, the patient was instructed to continue the therapy while
driving. Each time she would approach a red light, she would
begin the relaxation exercises and in this way avoid the fear
response. This in no way impaired her driving ability and helped
to transfer the learning acquired from the hierarchy to a real life
situation.

A six month follow-up showed that this patient continued to
make excellent progress towards resolving her phobic reaction. I
had spoken to the judge, and upon my recommendation, this
patient was allowed to keep her driver's license and received no
further traffic citations. The phobic reaction, which had generalized to red lights on emergency and police vehicles, disap-
peared completely when she recovered from her fear of lights at
intersections.

SEX AND FEAR

Over 70 percent of the gratification inherent in sexual activity
revolves around emotional reactions. Physical attraction and
sexual excitement are both stimulated by your emotions. This
fact may startle those of you who believed that sexual activity is
strictly a physical, touching activity. Bennett's case is a good
illustration of how fear can affect this delicate emotional balance,
which determines how well we perform sexually.

Bennett is a successful forty-eight-year-old man, who works as
a store manager for a large chain of department stores. New
regulations and increased demands from the home office caused
Bennett to experience high blood pressure. He went to his doctor,
who immediately put him on blood pressure medication. The
blood pressure medication worked fine to bring his blood pressure back within acceptable limits, but the side effect was devastating. From the fourth week of the medication, Bennett noticed
that he was unable to obtain and maintain an erection adequate to
engage in sexual intercourse with his wife. At first he was
dismayed and extremely fearful of the old wives' tale that he had
reached a certain point in his life and would not be able to perform

sexually. His impotency continued for the next three months. The more he tried to conquer the problem, the worse the situation became.

Tension between him and his wife was growing and she was at a loss to know what to do. He was able to hide the problem from everyone but his wife and himself.

Each day he experienced the nagging thoughts that he was less than a man and would never be able to satisfy his wife again. Up until this incident, their sexual relationship had been a very good and productive part of their marriage. Now the future looked bleak to say the least.

In desperation, Bennett went back to see his physician and to his dismay found out that one of the side effects of blood pressure medication was the possibility of secondary impotency. The physician gave him some instructions and reduced the dosage of medication. The amount of the drug which Bennett was taking was not sufficient to cause the impotency anymore.

Yet the problem persisted.

To put it very simply, Bennett had developed a fear reaction towards the impotency. He was so worried and concerned that he would not be able to perform, that he inadvertently caused the impotency despite the reduction in medication. During any sexual foreplay, he was fine and was able to maintain an erection, but immediately upon the thought of intercourse, he began to fear that the erection would disappear. As soon as he became fearful, the body reaction caused him to lose the erection.

It is known that in both men and women, the experience of fear can significantly hamper sexual activity and gratification.

Bennett's case is not in the least unusual. People, both men and women, who have had bad or frustrating sexual experiences, may develop a fear reaction towards sex and therefore receive no gratification from this activity. From the initial fear reaction, a chaining effect develops and very soon the individual has developed a phobic reaction towards sex.

Debbie feared sex in a different way. A marriage at age 18 lasted only a year and a half before divorce. At 25 she was still single. With a good job and positive outlook for the future, she should not have had any significant problems; but she could not develop and maintain a relationship with a man. No one seemed to meet her expectations and one disappointment followed another, causing her to dread getting involved with anyone. She found herself avoiding men and believing that she didn't really care about them. Her phobia towards the opposite sex was growing.

To understand Debbie's problem, it is necessary to look at her previous relationships with men. She had been serious about only one other boy before her early marriage. They had planned to get married, but their romance had been shattered by the shock of finding her boyfriend sleeping with her best friend. This shock was deepened by the fact that Debbie had staunchly resisted pre-marital sex during their relationship. A week before she found out about her best friend, Debbie had relented and had sexual relations with her boyfriend. The anger she felt upon discovering his deception was enormous.

It took her almost a year to get over the incident. Or so she thought.

The man she married had been very kind to her during their courtship, and she felt comfortable with him. Shortly after their marriage, however, she noticed a declining interest in sex and a real fear of having an orgasm. Eventually she started dreading the sexual part of the marriage. About a year later she discovered that her husband had been seeing several other women while away on business trips. The shock produced a near breakdown and was followed immediately by divorce.

Several years later Debbie was still afraid of men because she had developed a fear of being hurt. Each time in the past that she had been trusting, that trust had been broken. Since her mistrust of men was directly connected to sexual activity, she therefore feared that any sexual activity would make her vulnerable to hurt again. As a result, she closed herself off and developed a phobia towards relationships with the opposite sex. She was unhappy and floated in and out of depression, developing a compulsive avoidance pattern in order to protect herself from possible emotional hurt.

The fear of relationships with men had generalized to the point where she had difficulty even talking with men on a one to one basis. When she did date, she found herself cold and aloof. She was constantly looking for secondary motives in everything her dates said or did. This made the dating experience extremely unsatisfactory and difficult.

Debbie's reaction is not unlike that of many people today. Both men and women develop fear reactions as a protection against what they feel might be possible emotional hurt. Some of the walls we build around ourselves become so thick that after a period of time we are unable to see the reality of our situation. Debbie needed to overcome her fear of being intimately involved with a man. At the same time she had to realize that although no one can be guaranteed the outcome of a friendly relationship, one can increase the odds that a relationship will be productive and satisfactory by first reducing one's fear of the opposite sex and by having the courage to assert one's needs in a relationship. Fear can block communication and prevent each partner from knowing what the other one wants.

CHAPTER TEN
You've Only Just Begun

> *"But first of all let me assert my firm
> belief that the only thing we have to
> fear is fear itself—nameless, unreason-
> ing unjustified terror which paralyzes
> needed efforts to convert retreat into
> advance."*
>
> FRANKLIN D. ROOSEVELT,
> First Inaugural Address, March 4, 1933.

Although this is the last chapter of this book, it will be the first chapter in the search for your new fear-free life-style. The one point which has been stressed over and over again in this book, is that RESPONSIBILITY FOR SELF CHANGE IS YOURS.

A very common question, asked by many people who finish the phobia reduction program is, "How can I prevent fears from happening again?"

You will never be completely able to stop fears from occuring in your lifetime. Fears are a part of life experience. As we have seen, some fears are actually productive and should not be erased. Only irrational fears need to be extinguished. No one can guarantee that you will never experience another irrational fear.

But if you truly wish to change your behavior and eradicate fear, you can.

The methods outlined in this book do not guarantee that fears will not develop in the future. They are designed to help you deal effectively with fears and phobias which are presently affecting your lifestyle and could affect it in the future if they are not resolved. Of course, there will be some carry-over and you will be less likely to develop fear reactions in the future, after participating fully in this program.

TAKE A FEAR CHECK-UP

Some people feel that once fears have been identified through the checklist provided in this book, there is no reason ever to turn back to that chapter. This is incorrect. As we have explained, some fears develop blatantly with great fanfare and you are instantly aware of their presence. Other fears may develop more subtly and you may not be aware of them. This is why I recommend that at least once a year, you take time to re-do the checklist.

Just as you need a physical check-up or a dental check-up once a year you should also initiate a fear check-up.

FEAR REDUCTION PROGRAM CHECK LIST

Below is a step by step list of all the parts to the fear reduction program. Check each step as you complete it.

1. _____Read chapters One through Three
2. _____Fill out the *Fear Inventory* — Part A
3. _____Fill out the *Fear Inventory* — Part B
4. _____FEAR INTENSITY PROFILE
5. _____Chapter Five
6. _____Chapter Six
7. _____Chapter Seven
   - Part one
   - Part two
   - Part three

If your fear check-up indicates that new fears have evolved or an old fear has reared its ugly head again, then you should re-initiate the procedure of the fear reduction program.

TAKE THE TIME
There is a big surge nationwide to re-educate the public towards mental and physical preventive medicine. The same applies to the development of fears. Steps to help prevent their reoccurrence, and quick identification of new fear problems, are described below.

PRACTICE EVERY DAY
You should practice the relaxation exercises a minimum of ten minutes per day, every day. This means for the rest of your life, not just on those occasions when you are feeling distressed or caught up in the web of a fear reaction. True preventive medicine needs to be practiced every single day. As you become more proficient at the autogenic exercises, your time for initiating a relaxation response will be significantly shortened. For some people, who have practiced diligently, the time required to develop a relaxation response may be as short as 1½ minutes. If you stop and think about it, most of us waste at least forty-five minutes each day, usually more. If this wasted time were applied to maintaining mental and physical health, chances are you would be leading a much happier life.

LONG-TERM BENEFITS
The autogenic exercises may be used to improve certain levels of performance. As an example, if you are scheduled to play the piano in front of a group of people, use the autogenic exercises to calm yourself before you have to play. Suggestions such as, "my fingers know the music and I play in a calm and relaxed manner," can be used with the standard autogenic exercises. Use the breathing exercises while you are actually playing. If you notice a tight feeling in your neck or shoulders while you are in the middle of the music, simply let the muscles in your neck and shoulders relax through the autogenic phrases. If you have practiced every

day, these phrases will have become so ingrained that you will be able to perform them while involved in other activities. Of course, this level of sophistication takes some time to develop and should not be attempted unless you have fully mastered the autogenic-relaxation process. Many people have found the autogenic exercises to be extremely helpful in many types of sports activity.

A 44-year-old golfer found her game definitely improved after eight weeks of training. She also noted that repeating the phrase "my shoulders are heavy" before hitting the ball dispelled tension and added to the precision of her golf technique.

A 34-year-old judo enthusiast found that the regular practice of autogenic exercises helped him to react faster, remain calmer, improve his timing and retain vigor.

The autogenic exercises reduce tension, have a calming effect and improve nervous system and muscular coordination. For example, a 22-year-old singer practicing heaviness and warmth exercises found she was able to sing very fine and high notes during an exercise. Later, during practice periods, and actual stage performances, she mastered alto passages easily by thinking for a moment, "My hands are heavy."

It is felt that autogenic training stimulates brain discharges of neuromuscular activities. This helps the brain "unload" certain muscular activities in a self-curative process. Autogenic training also helps to neutralize repressed anxieties, in effect defusing potentially explosive aggression and bad memories.

Through a process of passive relaxation you gradually become less anxiety-ridden and less preoccupied with obsessive thoughts beyond your voluntary control.

Children treated with autogenics for stuttering and bed wetting become less irritable and moody, better behaved and less distractable at school as a result of reduced tension and nervousness. In some schools, teachers have experimented with autogenic training on an entire class, with favorable results, including improved intellectual functioning and improved classroom behavior.

In another case, a painter found her paintings somehow changed for the better following autogenic therapy, which allowed the creative process to grow from deep within her, rather than "making" her paintings as before.

Businessmen who wish to increase their efficiency, counterbalance the stress of office pressure, heavy responsibilities and long hours of monotonous work with unavoidable frustrations, have learned autogenic training. They often find themselves less irritable and friendlier in the office, more efficient and capable at their jobs.

Whether you use this method before serving in tennis or putting in golf, the more relaxed and coordinated your body is the better your performance. Passive concentration has been the key to many outstanding performances from bowling to playing bridge.

TELL YOURSELF THE TRUTH

Listen to what you are telling yourself. We all give ourselves messages and many times they are erroneous. Sort out the rational from the irrational inner talking. When you tell yourself that you are doomed to failure, there is a very good chance that your preoccupation with disaster may eventually lead to realization of your own self prophecy. Our body does what our brain tells it to and if we give it negative messages long enough, the body and mind will begin to react in a negative manner.

KEEP CHECKING

Use the checklist provided in this book to re-evaluate the status of your fear reactions. Lack of commitment to re-evaluate and practice daily forms the basic breeding ground for the development of new irrational fears.

STAND UP STRAIGHT

Be assertive. Stand up for what you believe in and go through with your decisions. Don't be afraid to ask yourself questions regarding your own behavior.

DON'T BE AFRAID TO SEE A DOCTOR

If your fear is in any way connected with a physical problem, you must see a doctor. The treatments outlined in this book will not heal a broken leg or change a bad heart valve, but when they are coordinated with medical treatment, they will serve to hasten the rate of recovery from certain medical procedures. The fear reduction program and autogenics are an invaluable aid towards reducing the chances of being stricken by the stress-related illnesses which tend to plague our present-day society.

BE YOUR OWN BEST SALESMAN

Never sell yourself short. It is within your ability to change the way you live your life. No one else can change it for you. You must take the initiative to learn the methods (as outlined in this book) and then follow through.

FOLLOW THROUGH
FOLLOW THROUGH

LOOK TOWARDS YOURSELF

Putting the blame for feelings of fear upon other people, situations or objects, is very common. Many people I know spend a considerable portion of their energies forming, manipulating and planning their life events in order to avoid taking the responsibility for their own actions. Placing the blame on somebody else for our own discomfort tends to be a dilemma of our society.

Take a few moments now and fill out the following questionnaire.

____• Airplanes make me scared
____• People scare me
____• Big animals are scary
____• Small bugs make me scared
____• Dark rooms make me scared
____• Not having money makes me fearful

_____• Being assertive makes me fearful
_____• Hypodermic needles give me an upset stomach

Look back over the list and see if you have put a check mark before any of the statements. If you have, then there is a great possibility that you are maintaining some of your fears under erroneous assumptions. These assumptions are that inanimate objects, situations, and other people have the power to cause you discomfort.

The Plain Truth Is That You Are the Cause of Your Own Discomfort

Let's take the example of a statement muttered by a 19-year-old girl:

"My Boss Makes Me Scared, Causes My Body to Tremble"

When I examine this statement, the basic falseness of the situation is quite obvious. If the statement were broken down into its component parts, we would readily see how ridiculous her assumptions are.

A. Her boss speaks to her in a certain manner or acts in a certain way which she perceives through her senses.

B. She hears his voice, sees the expression on his face, senses the tone of his statements, and maybe even senses certain smells.

C. All of this incoming information is immediately logged and catalogued within the cells of her brain.

D. A split second decision is made in her brain regarding her emotional response to the perceived situation. The emotional response may be derived from past experience, various aspects of her socialization, feelings about her own self worth and other psychological and emotional variables which are too numerous to mention.

E. She makes the decision to react in a specific manner.

The key to this whole sequence is that she, and only she, has made the decision regarding how she will interpret and react to a specific set of stimuli. In other words, he has not made her fearful, but the way she has interpreted his actions may elicit a fear response.

A fear response may be irrational or rational. Without exception, the idea that YOU MAKE THE DECISION ABOUT WHAT MAKES YOU FEARFUL could be one of the most important things you learn from this book.

Throughout your entire lifetime, you will be constantly bombarded with new experiences, thoughts and situations. No one can foretell the future and what may lie ahead. By maintaining a high level of proficiency in the relaxation-autogenic methods, you can immediately reverse the effect of any developing fear reaction. And since many fear reactions are learned and can therefore be unlearned, you can reverse the effects of ingrained fears also.

FEAR LIMITS FREEDOM

Follow the simple recommendations listed below and you will find that life will hold more enjoyment for you. You will be free to live a life in which you are not controlled by fear.

1. Be aware that the behavior of others may cause you to react with apprehension or fear.
2. Maintain a constant level of practice of relaxation-autogenic skills to control any anxiety or fear responses.
3. Try to rule out assumptions, based totally on your feelings, that something will go wrong in the future.
4. Be honest with yourself and admit when you are fearful. Admitting the problem to yourself has to be the initial step towards self-help procedures outlined in this book.
5. Do not let anyone else solve the problem for you. Remember that you *must take the responsibility to help yourself get better.*

Since this is the single most important concept in ensuring your success with this treatment program, let me repeat it:

You Must Be Willing to Take the Responsibility to Help Yourself Get Better

A commitment to help oneself solve one's own problems may have a greater impact upon long-term mental and physical health than any drug or surgical procedure now known.

FEARS CONTROL YOUR LIFE ONLY AS MUCH AS YOU ARE WILLING TO LET THEM

Each one of us, if we are truthful with ourselves, will admit to having experienced a fear at some time during our life. These fears may range from feelings of panic when boarding an airplane to the fear of childbirth. In these instances, fear and anxiety go hand in hand and lend themselves to the uncomfortable feelings experienced when we are fearful.

But don't try to erase *rational fears,* which may be useful and necessary in our natural growth process. The following represents a list of natural and, in some cases, productive fears:

RATIONAL FEARS
1. Putting your hand in a flame
2. Walking across a street in heavy traffic
3. Leaning too far over a cliff
4. Approaching a rattlesnake
5. Jumping into the deep end of a swimming pool without knowing how to swim
6. Driving with a person who has had many accidents
7. Taking unlabeled medications
8. Walking down a dark alley in an unfamiliar city

DON'T CLING TO INAPPROPRIATE FEARS

On the other side of the coin, we find irrational fears. These fears are maladaptive and do very little to help us enjoy life They are just like crab grass in your lawn. If you do not destroy them immediately, then they will grow and spread. Soon the crab grass begins to crowd out the good grass in your yard. The same thing happens with your personality, the way you think, and the way you act. Groupings of irrational fears (phobias) may crowd out all of the enjoyment and good parts of your life, only to leave a vast field of crab grass. A few examples of such phobias include:

1. The fear of riding in cars
2. The fear of being a passenger in a commercial airline
3. The fear of surgery by a qualified surgeon
4. The fear of flying insects
5. The fear of high places
6. The fear of injections
7. The fear of talking in front of a group
8. The fear of meeting new people

In many cases, ignoring irrational fears can be just as harmful as ignoring rational fears. If you are afraid of riding in cars, and are located in a big city where you only have to take the subway, then you have a built-in mechanism for avoiding the phobic situation. On the other hand, if you are in a situation that forces you to ride in cars on a regular basis, and you are afraid to do so, then you will develop the symptoms of a phobic reaction, which may interfere with your lifestyle. You must remember that avoidance is only a temporary mechanism. You must learn to eliminate your fears completely. If you only half bury a phobia, it will constantly reappear to haunt you later on, and make you very unhappy. Conscious or unconscious avoidance of fear-producing situations may cause emotional and physical unhappiness.

A considerable amount of time has been spent in this book pointing out what may happen if fears go unresolved. A number of emotional and psychological problems have been mentioned in previous chapters, but I think it is important to reiterate the premise that from unresolved fear reactions, numerous psychosomatic disorders can arise. By psychosomatic, I mean physical disorders for which no organic or physical reason can be found. A person suffering from a psychosomatic disorder may experience the physical symptoms just as strongly and as devastatingly as a person who actually has the organic disease.

Don't ever forget that continued fear reactions may cause undue stress and lead to problems such as stomach disorders, which occur because of blood being shunted away from the stomach under stressful or fear conditions. Remember that during stress there is a higher output of hydrochloric acid in the stomach and this may in turn produce severe indigestion and may eventually lead to ulcers. Fear can produce other digestive problems such as alternating diarrhea and constipation.

I've taken the digestive process as a small example, but don't kid yourself — psychosomatic dysfunctions occurring from fear reactions may touch upon every single part of your physical well-being.

LETHARGY

Many times I have found that people who are running away from their fears and developing psychosomatic disorders as a result of non-treatment, attempt to maintain such a "low profile" that they become extremely vulnerable to many of the negative life events they help set up for themselves, such as job loss, personal injury and financial and family loss.

Lethergy is not something that comes upon you all at once. It sneaks up like a snake in the dark. Be aware of it; don't let it take hold of you. Maintain a level of activity which will insure mental and physical fitness. Take up jogging, play ping-pong, play tennis, do anything, but keep active. Practicing your relaxation program and maintaining a good level of activity will be a better insurance policy for mental and physical health than money can buy. There is no insurance policy on the market today which can offer you as many benefits as are found in constructive physical activity and following the program as outlined in this book.

Remember, irrational fears will not go away by themselves. Like crab grass, they are very hard to kill and unless you get them by the roots, they will come back to affect your life again and again.

As a parting word, remember, we have to have the courage to let go of what we are now, in order to experience what we can become. Life is growth, but fear paralyzes growth. Only when you learn to free yourself from fear will you be able to experience the person you truly are. Remind yourself that unresolved fears get in your way and prevent you from reaching your goals.

Stop!

Remind yourself that you are feeling fear only because you are choosing to feel scared. This takes the responsibility off other people, events or objects, and puts the responsibility directly where it belongs:

On you!

Complete List of Phobias

air: aerophobia
animals: zoophobia
anything new: neophobia
bacilli: bacillophobia
bad men: pavor sceleris
barren space: cenophobia
bearing a monster: teratophobia
bees: apiphobia
being alone: autophobia
being buried alive: taphephobia
being enclosed: clithrophobia
being locked in: claustrophobia
being looked at: scopophobia
being touched: haptephobia
birds: ornithophobia
blood: hematophobia
blushing: ereuthophobia
brain-disease: meningitophobia
bridges: gephyrophobia
burglars: scelerophobia
carriages: amaxophobia
cats: ailurophobia
change: kainophobia
childbirth: maieusiophobia
choking: anginophobia
cold: cheimaphobia
color(s): chromatophobia

comet(s): cometophobia
confinement: claustrophobia
contamination: molysmophobia
corpses: necrophobia
crossing street: dromophobia
crowds: demophobia
cumbersome, pseudoscientific terms: hellenophobia
dampness: hygrophobia
darkness: achluophobia
dawn: eosophobia
daylight: phengophobia
death: thanatophobia
definite disease: monopathophobia
deformity: dysmorphophobia
demons: demonia
depth: bathophobia
devil: demonophobia
dirt: mysophobia
disease: nosophobia
dogs: cynophobia
dolls: pediophobia
dust: amathophobia
eating: phagophobia
electricity: electrophobia
emptiness: kenophobia
everything: panphobia
examination: examination phobia
excrement: coprophobia
eyes: ommatophobia
failure: kakorrhaphobia
fatigue: kopophobia
fearing: phobophobia
feathers: pternophobia
female genitals: eurotophobia
fever: fibriphobia
filth: mysophobia

filth (personal): automysophobia
fire: pyrophobia
fish: ichthyophobia
flash(es): selaphobia
flogging: mastigophobia
floods: antlophobia
flutes: autophobia
flying: airplane phobia
fog: homichlophobia
food: cibophobia
forest(s): hylophobia
frog(s): batrachophobia
functioning: ergasiophobia
ghosts: phasmophobia
girls: parthenophobia
glass: crystallophobia
God: theophobia
gravity: barophobia
hair: trichopathophobia
heat: thermophobia
heaven: uranophobia
height: acrophobia
hell: hadephobia
heredity: patriophobia
high objects: batophobia
house: domatophobia
ideas: ideophobia
infinity: apeirophobia
injury: traumatophobia
innovation: neophobia
insanity: lyssophobia
insects: acarophobia
jealousy: zelophobia
justice: dikephobia
knives: aichmophobia
large objects: megalophobia

left: levophobia
light: photophobia
lightning: astraphobia
machinery: mechanophobia
man: androphobia
many things: polyphobia
marriage: gamophobia
materialism: hylephobia
medicine(s): pharmacophobia
metals: metallophobia
meteors: meteorophobia
mice: musophobia
mind: psychophobia
mirrors: eisoptrophobia
missiles: ballistophobia
moisture: hygrophobia
money: chrematophobia
motion: kinesophobia
myths: mythophobia
naked body: gymnophobia
name: onomatophobia
needles: belonephobia
night: noctiphobia
northern lights: auroraphobia
novelty: kainophobia
odor (personal): bromidrosiphobia
odor(s): olfactophobia
open spaces: agoraphobia
pain: algophobia
parasites: parasitophobia
people: anthropophobia
places: topophobia
pleasure: hedonophobia
points: aichmophobia
poison: iophobia
poverty: peniaphobia

precipice(s): cremnophobia
punishment: poinephobia
rabies: cynophobia
railroad or train: siderodromophobia
rain: ombrophobia
rectal excreta: coprophobia
rectum: proctophobia
red: erythrophobia
responsibility: hypengyophobia
ridicule: catagelophobia
right: dextrophobia
river(s): potamophobia
robbers: harpaxophobia
rod: rhabdophobia
ruin: atephobia
sacred things: heirophobia
scabies: scabiophobia
scratches: amychophobia
sea: thalassophobia
self: autophobia
semen: spermatophobia
sex: genophobia
sexual intercourse: coitophobia
shock: hormephobia
sin: hamartophobia
sinning: peccatiphobia
sitting: thaasophobia
sitting down: kathisophobia
skin disease: dermatosiophobia
skin lesion: dermatophobia
skin (of animals): doraphobia
sleep: hypnophobia
small objects: microphobia
smothering: pnigerophobia
snake: ophidiophobia
snow· chionophobia

solitude: eremophobia
sounds: acousticophobia
sourness: acerophobia
speaking: lalophobia
speaking aloud: phonophobia
spider: arachneophobia
stairs: climacophobia
standing up: stasiphobia
standing up and walking: stasibasiphobia
stars: siderophobia
stealing: kleptophobia
stillness: eremiophobia
stories: mythophobia
stranger(s): xenophobia
street(s): agyiophobia
string: linonophobia
sunlight: heliophobia
symbolism: symbolophobia
syphilis: syphilophobia
talking: lalophobia
tapeworms: taeniophobia
taste: geumaphobia
teeth: odontophobia
tests: testaphobia
thinking: phronemophobia
thunder: astraphobia
time: chronophobia
travel: hodophobia
trembling: tremophobia
trichinosis: trichinophobia
tuberculosis: phthisiophobia
vaccination: vaccinophobia
vehicle: amaxophobia
venereal disease: cypridophobia
void: kenophobia
vomiting: emetophobia

walking: basiphobia
water: hydrophobia
weakness: asthenophobia
wind: anemophobia
women: gynophobia
work: ponophobia
writing: graphophobia